Understanding the Family Business

Understanding the Family Business

Exploring the Differences Between Family and Nonfamily Businesses

Second Edition

Keanon J. Alderson, MBA, PhD

BUSINESS EXPERT PRESS

Understanding the Family Business: Exploring the Differences Between Family and Nonfamily Businesses, Second Edition

Copyright © Business Expert Press, LLC, 2018.

First published in 2011 by
Business Expert Press, LLC
222 East 46th Street, New York, NY 10017
www.businessexpertpress.com

ISBN-13: 978-1-63157-573-0 (paperback)
ISBN-13: 978-1-63157-574-7 (e-book)

Business Expert Press Entrepreneurship and Small Business Management Collection

Collection ISSN: 1946-5653 (print)
Collection ISSN: 1946-5661 (electronic)

Cover and interior design by Exeter Premedia Services Private Ltd., Chennai, India

Second edition: 2018

10 9 8 7 6 5 4 3 2 1

Printed in the United States of America.

As always, to Sandy, and to my family

Abstract

The purpose of this book is to provide readers with an introductory overview of family business, the most prevalent form of business in the world. The differences between family and nonfamily businesses are emphasized in this book. This book has several key audiences and can be used as a supplemental text for university undergraduate or graduate level courses such as small business management, introduction to business, entrepreneurship, or family studies. Members of family businesses will benefit from the book as an introduction to the unique nature of family businesses. Professional advisors to family firms, such as accountants, attorneys, bankers, insurance providers, and financial services professionals, may develop a better understanding of their clients. Suppliers to family businesses will gain insight to this important business customer. Much of the literature on family business is from the United States; an attempt has been made to present relevant international information as well.

Chapter 1 defines and provides an overview of family business. Chapter 2 explores the many differences between a family-owned business and a nonfamily-owned business. Chapter 3 explores the major family business theories. Chapter 4 discusses how family firms make business decisions. Chapter 5 explores the significant issues prevalent in a family firm. Chapter 6 explores the most problematic issue in family firms: succession or the transfer of ownership to the next generation. Chapter 7 focuses on effective family business governance and use of advisors and boards. Chapter 8 explores key success tips for long-lasting family firms. Chapter 9 discusses trends and further research in family business.

Keywords

Family business, family-owned enterprise, family management, entrepreneur, entrepreneurship, entrepreneurial management, small business ownership, succession, intergenerational succession, conflict, siblings

Contents

List of Illustrations

Tables

Figures

Foreword

I grew up in a family business in South Africa (Bianchi Hotels [Pty] Ltd.) and have dedicated my entire life to family business. Family businesses make up between 70% and 92% of all businesses worldwide, varying between different cultures and countries. Nonetheless, the numbers are there and they are astounding. More than half the United States' gross domestic product is produced by family businesses, and they are the largest job creators (employers) in the nation.

Family businesses are unique in character and face many different and pertinent issues that are not encountered in corporate firms. Dr. Keanon Alderson depicts, in a very coherent and systematic way, the differences between family businesses and nonfamily businesses. Dr. Alderson comes from and has worked in his own family businesses, so his understanding of these pertinent issues is evident throughout this well–thought out book.

As a consultant to family businesses for the past 20 years and a lecturer at both the graduate and undergraduate level at San Diego State University, I find this book has been written with depth and understanding of the issues facing family businesses. It is an easy read, and students of family business will find it enlightening. This book will help the reader understand, appreciate, and differentiate between a family business and a nonfamily business. As Dr. Alderson says, "Family business is the most prevalent form of business in the world." I look forward to making this book available to all my students as we continue to create an awareness of the important role family business plays in our global economy.

Carmen Bianchi and Associates
Former Director, Entrepreneurial Management
Center (EMC) Business Forum
College of Business Administration
San Diego State University
Past President, The Family Firm Institute (FFI), 2007–2009

Preface

My experiences working in my family's manufacturing and distribution business for 17 years shaped my early life, and they continue to do so today. I was there at the conception of the company; I helped choose the company name and the colors of the packaging. When I was 15, I worked in the packaging department after school and on weekends (seven days a week *for free*). When I was 16, I received a raise to one dollar a day! This put $7.00 worth of gas in my VW van, enough for all week. One day, after a 24-hour period with no sleep (when we rushed out the largest order ever in order to make a deadline), I asked my father, "Why are we working so hard?" The answer was classic: "One day this will all be yours." It worked! There were no complaints from my brother or me, and the entire family buckled down, with the same goal of building the business to provide for our family and our future.

Our company rode the fast-growing trend of health and nutrition products in the 1970s and 1980s. We had tremendous growth, the management of which was an ever-present problem, albeit a great problem to have. One year, our sales increased 1,600%! Imagine the constant strain on cash. In the early 1980s, we received a buyout offer of over one million dollars. We really did not consider it for more than a few minutes. Our growth had no end in sight. Why sell out now? The members of our family made a very nice living. Let us keep this for our children and grandchildren, we thought. At our peak, we employed more than 65 people. I ran most of the sales force; my brother ran the manufacturing, packaging, and warehouse operations; and our father oversaw the company as a whole. Our mother worked off and on as needed. We each had our areas of expertise, yet when our roles overlapped, there could be some disagreement. For example, my father came from sales, so our roles overlapped often. My father had final decision-making authority, yet he listened to our input and desired consensus. After a few years, my brother and I became partners. We split equally one-third of the company; our parents had two-thirds.

In the late 1980s, we lost our largest customer, which had accounted for 30% of our sales. After a few rounds of pay cuts, and some serious belt tightening and hard work, we built the company back up to where it was previously. Eventually, the decision was made by all the family members to sell the firm. We all went our separate ways after working together for almost 20 years.

In many respects, being at the family business was the best of times. I miss the lightning-quick strategic decision making and implementation and the always-present entrepreneurial opportunities and risks. Along the way, there were long workdays, few vacations, discussions of business during holidays, some arguments, hurts, and conflicts of interest. The experience fueled my interest in studying the practice of family business, and in particular trying to discover what successful family firms do differently from others. Unfortunately, our family was not aware of family business consultants at the time. Looking back on the situation, I am left wondering whether we were as good as we thought we were or whether our success was simply due to being in the right place at the right time and riding the upward momentum of a large trend. Some key strategic decisions were eventful: Our decision to diversify away from our core competencies into manufacturing took a massive investment in raw materials and expensive increases in inventory, thus hurting the cash flow. The decision not to invest in other areas, such as real estate, when business was going exceptionally well could now be seen as shortsighted.

Our family business would have benefited from the advice, principles, and pearls of wisdom from research scholars and the successful family businesses presented in this book. It is my desire for this book to help other families in business. Families in business together need to know that issues will arise. It is a sad truth when the family business owner reads the Wall Street Journal or watches the financial news channels, they are not getting what they need to run their business. There is no focus on the unique and numerous family business issues. This book has tips and techniques to manage through them, better understand their cause, and ways to prevent some issues from occurring.

In the seven years since the first edition of this book, many things have changed regarding family business such as; the increase of families in business internationally, tax and estate planning issues, mergers, acquisitions, and many family firms accepting buyout offers. Some firms originally in the book are not family owned anymore. The profile of family business has grown through an increase of academic and professional research. This new edition will focus more on the numerous differences between family owned and controlled businesses and nonfamily businesses,

Keanon Alderson

January, 2018

Introduction

The vast majority of businesses in the world are owned or controlled by families. Family business is by far the most prevalent form of business in the world. As many as 80%–95% of all businesses in the United States are family owned or controlled. In Europe, the prevalence of family business is approximately 70%–80%. It is estimated as much as 75%–90% of firms in the Middle East are family owned. In Latin America, 70% of all firms are owned or controlled by families. The Australian economy is controlled by family firms, estimated at approximately 67% of all businesses and Asia is dominated by family firms, many of them Chinese family firms that are based in other countries.

It is estimated that family businesses in the United States accounted for up to 50% of all industrial purchasing and 50%–60% of the 2003 gross domestic product (GDP). Family businesses are responsible for the majority of jobs in the United States, including 85% of private-sector jobs and 86% of all jobs created in the last 10 years.[1] Approximately 40%–50% of employment in Europe is at family-owned or family-controlled firms.[2] Over one-third of the companies on the Standard & Poor's 500 index are family owned or controlled, as are one third of the firms on the *Fortune* 500. Even large corporations (some of them publicly listed on stock exchanges) such as Ford, Michelin, Enterprise Rent-A-Car, BMW, Tyson Foods, Cargill, and IKEA can be considered family businesses by being owned or controlled by families.

Family Owned versus Family Controlled

A definition of family business is provided in chapter one. However, for the purpose of simplification, consider a local entrepreneur who recognized an opportunity, started a business, found success, and now his children work in the business. The business is small by corporate standards, but since the founder owns 100% of the business it generates a healthy income for his family. This is family *owned*. The family *owns* the business.

Alternatively, consider that same entrepreneur who found success, and was able to scale their enterprise to a large number of locations and hundreds of millions of dollars in sales. In order to fuel continued growth, the family may decide to sell some shares of stock to a private equity firm or to the public (called going public, or an initial public offering). This would result in the family having less shares of stock in the firm, and thus less control by the founding family. They are now part owners of the business. The family may be the largest shareholder group, they would have more votes, and thus *control* the company. This is called family controlled rather than family owned. The family does not own it all anymore.

Despite the high prevalence of family business in the global economy, many business people in the United States consider family business in a negative manner and derisively call them "mom & pops." It is true: The vast majority of family firms are small businesses, and we have all shopped at their stores and bought their merchandise often without realizing they were family owned businesses. Yet numerous examples of highly successful family-owned businesses have a sustainable competitive advantage and dominate their markets, and many of them are well known to us. For example, in the classic business book *Built to Last*, approximately a third of the firms were owned or controlled by families.[3] A family firm in the United States, Cargill, has managed to grow into a giant multinational corporation employing 160,000 people, with sales of $116 billion, and it remains privately held by the Cargill and MacMillan families. According to a Boston Consulting Group study, more than 30% of all companies with sales over $1 billion, are family owned or family controlled businesses.[4]

Management guru Peter Drucker wrote about the vital role family businesses play in our economy and entrepreneurship.[5] Consider that most businesses start out as family businesses or utilize family resources.

In an analysis of the 2010 *Forbes* 400 Richest Americans, as many as 44% derived their fortune from owning, controlling, or receiving an inheritance from a family business.[6] As an example, the 200-year-old du Pont family fortune is now split among multiple family members who collectively own 15% of DuPont. Other examples of family fortunes based on family enterprises are the Rockefellers, the Rothschilds, the Guggenheims, the Oppenheimers, and the Onassis family. The world's largest retailer, and one of the largest corporations in the world, Wal-Mart, is controlled by the descendents of the founder, Sam Walton. If the entire Walton family fortune was combined, instead of being separated as a result of the inheritance upon the founders' passing, the combined wealth would surpass that of Bill Gates and it would be twice that of Warren Buffett.[7] The business magazine Forbes is in its 100th year of family ownership. The academic publisher Sage is family owned as well.

The belief that family business is small and unprofessional is not an absolute. The United States has 143 family businesses with sales of more than $1 billion. Table I.1 lists the world's largest family-owned firms (in dollars), with the percentage of control held by the family in 2009.

Legendary investor Warren Buffett believes family businesses have a distinct competitive advantage, and he has purposefully sought out and

Table I.1. World's Largest Family Firms and Percentage of Family Control

Sales rank	Company	Percentage of family control
1	Wal-Mart	Walton family owns 41%
2	Toyota Motor Corp	Toyoda family owns 2%
3	Ford Motor Co.	Ford family owns approximately 40% of voting shares
4	Koch Industries	Koch family owns 84% of America's largest private company
5	Samsung	Lee family controls 22%
6	ArcelorMittal	Mittal family owns approximately 50% of the world's largest steel company.
7	Banco Santander	Botin family owns 2.5%
8	PSA Peugeot Citroën	Peugeot family holds 42% of voting shares
9	Cargill	Cargill and MacMillan families own 85% of the 111 year old firm
10	SK Group	Chey family controls 71 affiliated firms
11	Fiat S.p.A.	Agnelli family owns 30%
12	LG Group	Koo and Huh families own 59%
13	BMW	Quandt family controls 47% of shares
14	Hyundai Motor	Chung family members control large group (*chaebol*) of interrelated firms
15	Robert Bosch GmbH	Bosch family owns 7% of shares, but family charitable foundation controls 92% of voting rights

Source: Pearl and Kristies (2009, spring).

bought many family companies. His purchases include Clayton Homes, the $4-billion purchase of Iscar Metalworking in Israel, Helzberg Diamonds, Ben Bridge Jewelers, and Nebraska Furniture Mart (the latter from the Blumkin family). Buffett specifically focuses on well-managed companies, and he likes key management to stay in place. Buffett lets management stay in control, and he has a very hands-off management style. This can be ideal for a family in business who wishes to sell yet remain involved. Clayton Homes looked at the transaction as a way to have a greater impact on their industry but still stay on and manage the firm.[8] Buffett was pivotal in the very secretive Mars family (Mars Candy) $22 billion takeover of family-owned Wrigley (chewing gum). Buffett invested $6.5 billion in the deal. He also bought 60% of the Pritzker family's Marmon Holdings Inc. (Hyatt Hotels) after an interfamily lawsuit and court-ordered breakup of the 100-plus-year-old company. He is presently looking at European family firms for purchase.

Considering that the majority of new ventures fail within 20 years of inception, a firm that has been in business for many generations is impressive. When we add the complex issues associated with family businesses, the success becomes doubly impressive. It may be beneficial for other firms to observe what family firms are doing right and emulate some of their practices. Family businesses fill a significant space in business ownership. These businesses, regardless of their size, have unique complexities, issues, and problems that nonfamily-owned enterprises simply do not encounter. Some examples of these issues are sibling rivalry, multigenerational succession, nonworking family members, divorce, familial interpersonal conflict, and inheritance tax issues that face the ever-expanding generations of family members. For a family business to have faced those types of complex issues and still be thriving multiple generations later is a situation worthy of examination if not emulation. It is interesting to speculate on what a nonfamily business can learn from a family business.

CHAPTER 1

An Overview of the Family Business

Common Misconceptions of Family Businesses

Business historian Alfred Chandler assigned blame for the economic decline of Great Britain on family businesses. He described them as backward and small scale, with an inability to preserve financial capital.[1] Many still hold this negative view today. Many of the terms used when discussing family businesses can be condescending: small, unprofessional, rife with conflict, unable to compete, nepotistic, often failing to succeed, financially underperforming, unfavorable work environments, slow growing, and supplying of dead-end jobs.

Critics cite the high failure rate of intergenerational transfer (succession) as evidence that family businesses are not well-run businesses. Some of this criticism is well founded: Family businesses can be unprofessional. Many people have witnessed a small family-owned business in which one family member berates another family member in front of customers or has acted in an unprofessional manner. This book will discuss each of the misconceptions and will present differing, and often contradictory, information for readers to compare and consider.

Definition of the Family Business

A family business can be defined in multiple ways. There may be as many as 34 definitions.[2] The variety of definitions makes comparisons and generalizations difficult, which is a large part of the reason for the varying reports of levels of financial return and the contribution from family businesses to the economy. The breadth of definitions complicates having an accurate number of family businesses in the United States and the world. The following are a few of the various definitions of family business:

> A family member is chief executive, there are at least two generations of family control, a minimum of five percent of the voting stock is held by family or trust interest associated with it.[3]

> One in which a family has enough ownership to determine the composition of the board where the CEO and at least one other executive is a family member, and where the intent is to pass the firm on to the next generation.[4]

> The family business is a business governed and/or managed with the intention to shape and pursue the vision of the business held by a dominant coalition controlled by members of the same family or a small number of families in a manner that is potentially sustainable across generations of the family or families.[5]

Erenesto J. Poza, in his widely used text *Family Business*,[6] defined family business as

1. ownership control (15% or higher) by two or more members of a family or a partnership of families;
2. strategic influence by family members on the management of the firm, whether by being active in management, continuing to shape culture, serving as advisors or board members, or being active shareholders;
3. concern for family relationships;
4. the dream (or possibility) of continuity across generations.

The need for a universally accepted definition of family business was exemplified in the research of Astrachan and Shanker,[7] which assessed the contribution of family businesses to the U.S. economy. Family firms make up 24.2 million businesses in the country, accounting for 89% of all year 2000 tax returns, according to their broad definition of what constitutes a family firm. Conversely, in a more narrow definition, there are only 3 million family firms, accounting for 11% of all year 2000 tax returns.[8]

The definition of what is, and what is not a family firm is vital for family businesses and practitioners—not just for family business scholars. For the family to take advantage of the scholarly research, the discipline must be grounded in a common definition; otherwise, it is a little like comparing apples to oranges. For example, the small corner store has different problems, issues, and opportunities than Wal-Mart has, yet both are considered family firms.

The definition used in this book will be the broadest possible in order to provide an overview of the subject matter. Two things are important: More than one family member is involved in the firm as an owner, and the family exercises some type of control. This definition allows us to discuss the more prevalent small family-owned businesses as well as giant family-controlled multinational firms.

Prevalence of Family Businesses in the Global Economy

Family businesses are present in every country around the world. Often, family firms collectively dominate the economy of their particular country or region. This is the case in Latin America and South America, where *groupos* are prevalent and account for a majority of the gross domestic product (GDP). A groupo can be defined as an intertwined group of companies controlled by a large interrelated group of family members with key family and kinship partnerships. Since the markets of each country are relatively small in South America and Latin America, a family business often comes to dominate a certain industry, with a significantly large share of its particular country's market. To support the growing family, the decision is often made to diversify, usually vertically or horizontally, by buying suppliers or distributors. The firm then puts family members in control of the new organization. The result is a large web of closely related but tightly knit firms, who, in effect, are controlled by the original founding family.

In Japan, the large family-controlled *zaibatsus*, such as Matsushita and Sumitomo, were the dominant form of business in the first part of the 1900s until World War II when they were broken up by the government. These family firms evolved into interrelated *keiritsu*, a type of holding company usually dominated by a bank. One of Japan's biggest companies, Toyota, is controlled by the Toyoda family. In Korea, the economy is dominated by *chaebols* (large interrelated groups of firms) such as Samsung and Hyundai. Indonesia is dominated by family-owned *enterprise groups*. Many European economies rely on family-owned businesses and financing from banks, as the capital markets and access to venture capital are less developed than in the United States. The European stock exchanges are typically dominated by large, well-established corporations, which make up only a small part of Europe's economies. As an example, family-owned businesses with less than 500 employees (called *mittelstands*) account for 79% of the employment in Germany. Sweden's economy is dominated by a single family. In the 1990s, the Wallenberg family controlled almost 40% of the shares traded on the Stockholm stock exchange. In the 1970s, more than 10% of all private-sector employees worked for a Wallenberg company.

In many high-growth emerging markets, family-owned firms dominate and are especially beneficial to the industrialization and early-stage development of the country's economic infrastructure. Many family firms hold dominant places in the channel of distribution as middlemen or wholesalers. Due to their usual flat organizational structure, owner-managed firms do not have the layers of management bureaucracy that nonfamily firms have, and they can make rapid decisions to enter a market, finance an expansion or acquisition, or make a divesture without taking up valuable time. This allows family firms to enter an emergent market with a first-mover advantage, establish distribution, and tie up valuable resources, which can lead to a sustainable competitive advantage.

John D. Rockefeller, founder of Standard Oil, was the world's first billionaire. He monopolized the location, production, and distribution of oil and kerosene. His son, John D. Rockefeller Jr., is credited with creating the modern process of philanthropy, as we know it today, by establishing the Rockefeller Foundation. Family firms have played a more important role in the global economy as bankers. Both the Morgan and the Rothschild families have hundreds of years of experience in investment banking and financial services. The Rothschild's family financed the creation of De Beers (diamonds) and became a large stockholder in it. Powerful J. P. Morgan was instrumental in preventing the U.S. financial system from failure before the creation of the Federal Reserve System.

In addition to the United States, the prevalence of family business in countries and regions around the world is sizable. Their impact on employment and their countries' economic output is considerable, as shown in Table 1.1.

Table 1.1. Country and Prevalence of Family Business Around the World

Australia	67% of Australian companies are family businesses.[a]
Austria	Approximately 80% of all Austrian businesses are family controlled, employing between 70% and 75% of all employed Austrians.[b]
Belgium	83% of Belgium businesses with at least 5 employees are considered to be family owned in terms of one family possessing majority of ownership and perceiving the business as a family business.[c]
Brazil	The majority of Brazilian businesses are family owned, with as many as 90% family owned or controlled.[d]
Canada	Approximately half of the Canadian workforce is employed by a family business, accounting for nearly 45% of Canadian GDP.[e]
Chile	• Approximately 65% of all the firms in Chile are family owned or controlled.[f] • Family-controlled businesses on the Chilean stock exchange outperform their nonfamily-controlled counterparts.[g]
China	• As of 2009, the private sector represented 95% of all companies in China, the vast majority are family controlled, and most of the remaining firms are state-owned enterprises.[h] • The rural areas are heavily populated by small family farms.
Colombia	Family-owned or controlled firms constitute 70% of Colombian companies and range from small businesses to large *groupos.*[i]
Croatia	Approximately half of Croatia's employment is created by family businesses, 77% of which are managed by the owning families with no outside employees or management.[b]
Cyprus	Approximately 85%–90% of all businesses are family firms. They create approximately half of the country's employment and gross domestic product.[b]
Czech Republic	80%–95% of all businesses operating in the country can be classified as family businesses.[b]
Estonia	90% of all Estonian companies are family owned, accounting for approximately half of the country's employment.[b]
Finland	More than 90% of all Finnish businesses can be categorized as a family business, employing more than 40% of the country's workforce and accounting for 40% of Finnish national turnover.[j]
France	83% of French businesses are categorized as family businesses, employing almost half of the French workforce.[k]
Germany	• The 50 largest German family businesses outperformed the DAX (German stock index) by an average of 6.8% from 2003 to 2008.[l] • 84% of German firms are classified as family businesses.[d]

Greece	Families control approximately 80% of all Greek businesses.
Hungary	About 70% of all Hungarian businesses are family controlled, contributing to more than half of the country's employment.[b]
Iceland	Between 70% and 80% of all Icelandic businesses are considered family companies, employing up to 80% of the national workforce and creating 60%–70% of the national turnover.[b]
India	• Family businesses account for as much as 95% of all Indian businesses. • Nearly 80% of family owned companies in India dominate the Indian economy.[m] • As many as 461 of the 500 most valuable Indian companies are under family control.[n]
Ireland	• Almost half of all Irish businesses are family companies, providing 39% of all employment and producing nearly 30% of national turnover. • 33% of Irish capital acquisitions in the service sector were made by family businesses in 2005.[o]
Israel and the Middle East	• Around 75% of the Middle East's private economy is controlled by 5,000 wealthy families. These families account for 70% of the region's employment. • Family businesses control over 90% of commercial activity.[p] • With charity as a requirement of Islam, business families in the Muslim-Arab world have begun to structure their charitable endeavors to improve their support of the poor.[q]
Italy	• Up to 73% of all Italian businesses are family controlled, employing more than half of all employed Italians.[b] • Italy has the highest number of members in the Hénokiens Association, family companies older than 200 years that are still managed and largely owned by the original founding family.
Japan	• Family firms account for 96.5% of the total number of firms in Japan and also account for over 75% of total employment.[r] • Currently, the oldest family business in the world[s] is operating in Japan and is managed by the 46th generation of the founding family. • Family businesses tend to outperform nonfamily companies in most Japanese industries. • 42% of firms on the Japanese stock market are family owned or controlled.[t]
Lithuania	Family firms are increasing in prevalence since the fall of communism, now at about 38%. They contribute nearly 15% of gross domestic product.[b]
Luxembourg	Family businesses account for up to 70% of all businesses in Luxembourg.[b]
Mexico	Approximately 95% of the firms are family owned or controlled, accounting for 46% of the stock market.[u]
The Netherlands	74% of the country's firms are family businesses.[d]

Norway	Family businesses account for almost 66% of Norwegian private enterprise, creating around 40% of total employment.[b]
Portugal	Approximately 70%–80% of Portuguese businesses are family controlled, accounting for about half of the country's employment and creating two-thirds of the national turnover.[b]
Romania	About 20% of Romania's employment is created by family businesses[b]
Singapore	On average, family firms in Singapore are relatively small; they employ between 10 and 100 people, but make up 80%–90% of all industrial companies.[v]
Slovakia	Approximately 80%–95% of all Slovakian businesses can be categorized as family controlled.[b]
Slovenia	Approximately 60%–80% of all Slovenian businesses are family owned, employing 26% of the active workforce.[b]
South Africa	• A minimum of 1.1 million of the 1.4 million businesses in the country are family controlled.[w] • Approximately 80% of businesses in South Africa could be classified as family business.[x]
Spain	Approximately 75% of Spanish businesses can be categorized as family owned. They account for 65% Spain's GDP.[d]
Sweden	79% of Swedish firms are considered family owned.[d]
Turkey	Up to 90% of Turkish businesses are classified as family businesses.[b]
United Kingdom	Almost one-third of all UK employees work in family-owned businesses. They account for 65% of all UK businesses and contribute up to 40% of GDP.[e]

Notes. Adapted from Family Firms Institute (n.d.).

[a.] KPMG (2009).
[b.] Overview (2008).
[c.] Jorissen, Laveren, Martens, and Reheul (2005).
[d.] Family businesses (2003).
[e.] PricewaterhouseCoopers (2007/2008).
[f.] Family Firms Institute (n.d.).
[g.] Martinez et al. (2007, June).
[h.] Amit et al. (2010).
[i.] Berdugo and Cáceres (2010).
[j.] Aminoff et al. (2006).
[k.] FBN International (2007).
[l.] Family Firms Institute (n.d.).
[m.] Sanyal and Dutt (2010).
[n.] Tripathi (1999).
[o.] Birdthistle and Fleming (2007).
[p.] Open innovation (2010).
[q.] Family business (2007).
[r.] Goto (2005).
[s.] Kristies (2008).

Readers will no doubt be familiar with many of the well-known firms and brands that are family owned around the world (see Table 1.2).

Table 1.2. Well-Known Family Businesses Around the World

Australia	• Australia Zoo • News Corp. (founded)
Austria	• RedBull • Swarovski Crystal
China	• Li-Ka-Shing Holdings • Hutchison Whampoa/Cheung Kong • Sun Hung Kai Properties Ltd. • Swire Pacific Ltd. (Cathay Pacific)
Denmark	• Lego
France	• Carrefour • Chateau Lafite Rothschild • Dassault Aviation • Groupe Auchan S.A. • Groupe Danone • Hermès • L'Oréal • LVMH Moët Hennessy Louis Vuitton • Michelin • PPR (Gucci, Puma) • PSA Peugeot Citroën • Sodexo
Germany	• Adidas • Aldi • Bertelsmann • BMW • Boheringer Ingelheim • Bosch • Henkel • Merck • Metro • Porsche • Siemens AG
Greece	• Onassis
India	• HCL • Tata Group • Reliance • The Wadia Group
Indonesia	• Salim Group

Israel and the Middle East	• Al Fahim Group (Abu Dhabi) • Al Muhaidib Group (Saudi Arabia) • Elite Food • Strauss Investment • Jashanmal National Company (Dubai) • Nuqul Group • Saudi bin Ladin Group • Taybeh Brewery (Palestinian) • YBA Kanoo Shipping • Zamil Group Holding Co. (Saudi Arabia)
Italy	• Alessi S.p.A. • Barilla (pasta) • Benetton • Beretta • Ferrero • FIAT • illy • Prada • Salvatore Ferragamo Italia
Japan	• Ito-Yokado (7-11 Stores) • Kikkoman • Mori • Otsuka Pharmaceutical Group • Suntory Ltd. • Toyota
Korea	• Korean Air • LG • Samsung • Hyundai
Mexico	• Cemex • José Cuervo • Groupo Bimbo • Groupo Televisa
The Netherlands	• Heineken
The Philippines	• Ayala Corporation • SM Group
Scotland	• W. L. Grant (Glenfiddich)
Singapore	• Eu Yan Sang • Hong Fok Corporation • Lum Chang Holdings • United Overseas Bank

Spain	• Camper • El Corte Ingles • Roca • SCH (Banco Santander Central Hispano S.A.)
Sweden	• H&M (Hennes & Mauritz AB) • IKEA • Tetra Laval (Tetra Pak)
Switzerland	• Hoffman-La Roche Ltd. • Swatch • Union Bancaire Privée
South Africa	• De Beers
Taiwan	• Cathay Life Insurance • Fubon Financial Holding Co.
Thailand	• Charoen Pokphand Group (CP)
United Kingdom	• Anglo American mining • Associated British Foods • AstraZeneca PLC • J. Barbour & Sons • Sainsbury's
United States	• Alberto Culver • American Greetings • Campbell Soup • Cargill • Fidelity Investments • Ford Motor Company • Hallmark Cards • Hasbro • Hilton • Imperial Holly Sugar Co. • L. L. Bean • Marriott Corporation • Mars • Oreck • Wal-Mart

Note. Adapted from Family Firm Institute (n.d.)

CHAPTER 2

Differences Between Family and Nonfamily Firms

Several significant differences are apparent between family and nonfamily firms. Family businesses often have a long-term view; a lasting mission, vision, and purpose; a desire to create a nurturing, caring community and to act as stewards; and an ability to build relationships, bonds, and connections with customers, suppliers, and other outsiders.[1]

The Family

By far, the greatest difference between a family firm and a nonfamily firm is the addition of the family unit. The involvement of family is both an advantage and a disadvantage. It not only can lead to a tremendous competitive advantage but also can be the cause for serious dysfunction and complications. The nonfamily firm does not have to deal with many of the complex issues that family firms face, such as the upheaval of divorce, interpersonal conflict, inheritance and tax issues, and nonemployed family members with decision authority. Consider working for a family member you do not respect. Or one who is incompetent, but to complain would cause an irreparable rift in the family. Consider, for a minute, your life's work, your employment, and your wealth, all intermingled with your extended family.

The characteristics of families include an inward focus, unconditional acceptance, sharing, and the offer of lifetime membership. Families are based on love and are often very emotional. Conversely, businesses look outward, are based on tasks, and are unemotional. They embrace and encourage change and they reward performance: the accepted philosophy is "perform or leave." The two systems of organization are diametrically opposed to each other.

The family plays a dual role. First, they are a family, with the same kinds of similar issues and concerns as everyone else, such as what's for dinner, getting the kids to school and soccer practice on time, and poor old Uncle Joe's drug problem. Management becomes complicated when the family is involved in the business. Family issues or stresses may be brought to the business and vice versa. Now the usual concerns of business, such as money, investment, finances, employment, livelihood, and reputation, intertwine with the family. If Uncle Joe has a drug problem, it now affects the business as well as the family.

The family-owned business has complex family dynamics at work. Within the family business, conflicts can grow and become exaggerated. Communication within families is less formal than it is in professional settings. Some families communicate with respect, understanding, love, and compromise. Other families communicate by arguing, slinging accusations, and displaying feelings of distrust, dislike, and jealousy. Family business can be like a marriage: The parties can bring some baggage to the union. Instead of cooperating with each other, some family members constantly bring up unresolved issues and conflicts that have bruised their egos from early childhood.

Priorities

Family firms have different priorities than nonfamily firms have. Family businesses are associated with several nonfinancial objectives. Family companies are more likely to be concerned with the stability and continued family ownership of the business. Families often see employing family members as a priority. Families are less likely to seek rapid growth by selling equity, either privately or on the stock exchange. Families are not quick to lay off either family or nonfamily members. Families usually live and work in the same area, and their identity is often tied up in the business. They get a sense of satisfaction by employing members of their community. Often, their priorities are social or community related rather than strictly business or financial. In a long-standing firm, the family legacy is vitally important.

Values and Mission

In many companies, the mission statement is an unimportant but required component of a business plan. New business start-ups often write some platitudes that sound good to investors, such as caring for the community, the employees, and the environment. Once the mission statement is complete, they move on to the "more important business."

In practice, the mission of a company is vital to the success of the organization. The great power of the mission statement is its use as a decision-making tool: an aid to the employees and members of the firm. It discusses the purpose of the firm and why the firm exists. Why is it different from other firms? What does the company stand for? When employees and others know the underlying mission of the firm, they can make decisions on their own in the absence of managerial supervision. It keeps every employee moving in the same direction. If, for example, the firm stands for the highest levels of customer service, fairness, ethical standards, and quality, an employee should feel empowered to decide to stop the shipment of subpar merchandise that violates the mission of the organization. Families in business need to discuss and decide the important topics: Why are they in business together? Does the family business exist solely to make money? Or does it also exist to provide jobs for family members and the community? Does it exist to carry on the legacy and goals of the founder? Is there an altruistic element to its purpose, such as employing family members or providing employees with more benefits than competing companies?

In family businesses, the mission and values of the firm are a major differentiating factor from nonfamily businesses. Family firms commonly act altruistically with customers, employees, and the local community, and they often make decisions that do not maximize profitability in the short run.

Family businesses care about their family's legacy. Successive generations are concerned with the reputation of the family within the community, and they strive to honor the original mission and values created by the founders. For a family business, the mission statement and its corporate values are highly significant and very powerful.

The following are selected examples of family business mission and values statements:

- SC Johnson

  Employees: We believe that the fundamental vitality and strength of our worldwide company lies in our people.

  Consumers and users: We believe in earning the enduring goodwill of consumers and users of our products and services.

  General public: We believe in being a responsible leader within the free market economy.

  Neighbors and hosts: We believe in contributing to the well-being of the countries and communities where we conduct business.

  World community: We believe in improving international understanding.[2]

- Chick-fil-A's mission statement is be America's best quick-service restaurant at winning and keeping customers. Its corporate purpose is "to glorify God by being a faithful steward of all that is entrusted to us; and to have a positive influence on all who come in contact with Chick-fil-A." The family and the organization stay true to the founder's Christian principles; all restaurants are closed on Sundays.[3]

- Enterprise Rent-A-Car founder Jack Taylor described his business philosophy in this simple statement: "Take care of your customers and your employees first, and the profits will follow." The company has detailed its values into the following guiding principles:

  o Our brands are the most valuable things we own.

  o We do business every day as if our success depends on our company's good name—because it does. Our reputation and the powerful brands we build together are our most precious assets. Enterprise Holdings is a world-class company that was built by our employees—one transaction, one handshake, one kept promise at a time. That makes employees owners of our corporate identity and our service brands. In the marketplace and the communities we serve, they have the power to advance our standing and our reputation, one customer at a time.

o Personal honesty and integrity are the foundation of our success.

o As the personal face of our company to our customers and in our communities, our employees accept responsibility for demonstrating our true commitment to the highest ethical standards. We build loyal, long-term relationships with our customers and neighbors by treating them fairly, meeting their needs and earning their trust. These relationships, sustained by personal honesty and integrity, are the foundation of our success.

o Customer service is our way of life.

o We maintain an uncompromising commitment to customer service across each of our service brands, from our focus on complete customer satisfaction to directly linking career advancement opportunities to the actual level of service we provide. Customers seek us out— and stay with us—because we truly believe in and deliver a great customer experience. Our goal is simple but powerful: to exceed every customer's expectations.

o Our company is a fun and friendly place, where teamwork rules.

o We work hard to meet our goals for growth and success. But we work just as hard to keep our workplace enjoyable. Even in his late 8-'s and early 90's Jack Taylor still greeted his employees with the question, "Are you having fun?" We are known for our enthusiasm, high energy, healthy competitive drive and team spirit. As we continue to grow, we understand we can best fuel our collective success with a workforce that is upbeat, motivated and highly committed to each other's success.

o We work hard . . . and we reward hard work.

o Learning how to run a successful business from the ground up and delivering our high standard of service is hard work. It's work that demands a deep personal commitment from each employee. But Enterprise Holdings is also a true meritocracy that rewards this commitment personally, professionally, and financially by providing employees with ample opportunities for growth. We provide a solid foundation in business operations and true entrepreneurship that few, if any, companies offer. That makes Enterprise Holdings a great fit for career-minded individuals who take real ownership of, and responsibility for, their goals and aspirations.

o Great things happen when we listen . . . to our customers and to each other.

o We have learned that when we truly listen to our customers and understand their needs, they lead us to opportunities—from little ways to serve them better, to new lines of business that open up exciting growth prospects for our company. We listen carefully to one another, too. Day-to-day, face-to-face, listening leads us to working more effectively together. At Enterprise Holdings, we understand that an open and respectful exchange of ideas is critical to maintaining our high standards for service and personal success.

o We strengthen our communities, one neighborhood at a time.

o Our company has a presence in thousands of communities, placing us on a first-name basis with the people who call those communities home. We purchase millions of dollars worth of vehicles locally, generate tax dollars through sales and employment, create meaningful jobs that generate significant income and benefits for employees and their families, and much more. We realize we owe our success to the support and goodwill of the people who live in those communities and who do business with us. That's why we are committed to involving ourselves in the support of worthwhile endeavors wherever we operate our businesses, from local neighborhoods to the biggest cities and everywhere in between.

o Our doors are open.[4]

Goals

Like other firms, family businesses have multiple goals and objectives. However, a key difference is that family firms often have noneconomic goals. This is unlike the strictly profit-oriented beliefs suggested by economist,[5] who espoused that a corporation's sole purpose for existence is to increase shareholder wealth (stockholder approach).

Many family firms seem to embrace a different goal than profit maximization; that of the stakeholder approach.[6] This approach recognizes the business has many people who have a *stake* in the success or failure of the firm. These constituents include, stockholders, employees, customers, suppliers, the local community, and yes, even the government and the competition. The stakeholder approach treats each of these constituencies with respect and fair dealing. Family owned businesses are known for their fair dealing and this has led to the high amount of trust placed in them.

Long-Term Viewpoint

Several significant differences are apparent between family and nonfamily firms. One of the most readily apparent is the long-term outlook of family firms. Most family businesses seek to keep the business in the family and pass it on to the next generation. The American Family Business Survey[7] found that 85% of the firms surveyed wanted to continue with family ownership. The Laird Norton Tyee (LNT) Family Business Survey[8] found that 55% of the senior generation wanted successive generations to take over and almost 85% of family businesses who had chosen a successor chose a family member to carry on the business.[9]

Family firms have significantly longer time horizons than nonfamily firms. A Swedish study reported family firms had a longer life span than nonfamily firms: 37 years versus 22 years. Families remained the principle owners of a business for almost 30 years, compared with 12–13 for nonfamily firms.[10] Due to the average family CEO tenure of 24 years, compared to 3–4 years for nonfamily firms, family firms have no need to maximize short-term gains at the risk of long-term gains.[11] They can make decisions that will affect the firm years later and generations in the future. Due to the shorter CEO tenure in nonfamily firms, especially public firms, nonfamily management often emphasizes short-term results. They are concerned with increasing the price of the company stock, providing an excellent return for investors, and maximizing profitability in the short run. This very often translates into quarter-by-quarter short-term thinking, which can have significant negative effects on the long-term financial health of the firm.

A negative issue associated with long-term family tenure is referred to as *CEO entrenchment*. In some firms, a company with a long-serving CEO can become conservative, moribund, and stuck in its ways, and it may miss opportunities for growth and expansion. For these reasons, professional and highly functioning family firms utilize good governance procedures, such as a board of directors to guard against CEO entrenchment and other negative issues that can result from long-term tenure.

An association of family and bicentenary companies, the Association les Hénokiens formed in 1981 to honor and celebrate their members' long-standing family heritage. The association has 40 members: 14 Italian, 12 French, 5 Japanese, 3 German, 2 Dutch, 2 Swiss, 1 Belgian, and 1 from Northern Ireland. To become a member of the Hénokiens Association, a firm must have a minimum age of 200 years and the family must still own the company or be a majority shareholder. A relative of the founder must still manage the company or be on the board of directors. The company must also be in good financial health. The final requirement is being modern and up to date. Members of the organization include Fabbrica d'armi Pietro Beretta S.p.A., the large Italian firearms company, now in its 16th generation, and Netherlands-based liquor maker De Kuyper, which is now run by a 10th- generation family member.[12]

The British have a dozen firms in the Tercentenarian Club. The requirement is member firms must be over 300 years old, and still owned by the founding family. What these firms have achieved is impressive; they have survived 47 recessions, several banking crises, stock market crashes, the start of the Industrial Revolution and the end of using horses for power, two world wars, the defeat of Napoleon, and the creation and rise of the internet.[13] What we can learn from these successful and long lasting firms is nothing short of amazing considering all the challenges they have overcome.

Trust

A major component of the family business's competitive advantage is the high levels of trust among the family members, as well as customers, suppliers, and employees. Among family members the trust is relational and interpersonal and is founded on connections that are significantly deeper than the sheer economics of the business. The stronger foundations of trust include shared common experiences, common family characteristics, shared family identity, and history, as well as a united value system and mutual goals. Trust is usually greater among family members than among nonfamily members or when compared with nonfamily firms. When trust is not sustained over time, conflict increases and management (agency) costs rise.

High levels of trust have been shown to be vital for consumers and suppliers as well. Family businesses are seen as being more trustworthy than nonfamily firms (75% to 59%).[14]

Trust of family businesses is high among the customers, suppliers, community, and the employees. According to an eleven country survey, the general public's trust of family owned businesses is 75% vs only 59% in nonfamily firms. The public believes family firms have higher quality products and services at 51% to only 34% for non family firms. Family firms are perceived to listen to their customers at a higher rate, 50% for family firms vs 32% for nonfamily firms. A large 66% of consumers are willing to spend more at a family business than a nonfamily business.[15] This is a large competitive advantage for the family business.

Business Size

Data on family business size varies by country, depending on the tax policies and inheritance regulations. However, most family firms are small, with many fitting in the small and medium enterprise size. Several countries have a significant number of family businesses that also rank as some of the countries' largest businesses. The United States, Germany, and France all have extremely large family firms within their borders (see Table 1.2). The United Kingdom, conversely, does not have many large family firms, which is thought to be caused by tax and inheritance issues acting as barriers. Government and policy makers should be knowledgeable and aware of what is needed to properly support family firms in their country because of the substantial contributions of such companies to the overall economy.

Industry and Location

Throughout the world, family firms predominate in certain industries, such as service industries, agriculture, fishing, forestry, hotels, restaurants and catering, and distribution. Most family firms are not heavily represented in highly capital-intensive industries, such as finance, banking, and insurance firms. In the less developed economies, many families operate small farms. In the American Family Business Survey (2002), nearly a quarter of respondents (24.5%) were in the manufacturing industry. More than a sixth (16.6%) specialized in wholesale and distribution, 12.2% were in construction, and 11.1% were in retail. The rest of the industries combined—agriculture and forestry, financial services, high technology/biotechnology, mining/oil and gas, real estate, telecommunications and transportation—together accounted for 35.6% of family businesses responding to the survey.[16]

Family firms often cluster together, usually due to the specific industry they are involved in. The concentrations of these locations vary by country. In most countries, because of the high prevalence of family-owned farming businesses, family firms are overrepresented in rural areas.

Altruism

One of the most puzzling aspects for nonfamily firms and business professionals to understand about family-owned firms is their altruistic behavior. Often family firms break the rules of normal accepted business practices of profit maximization. For example, they may keep a trusted long-term employee past their prime, avoid needed layoffs to support the local community, or pay employees more than their earned contribution. It often amazes and frustrates consultants and advisors when a family firm does not want to follow through on recommendations that are fiscally sound and responsible. The family balks at the suggestions based on their stated mission and values and altruistic behavior. The cultural norms concerning the respect and role of family in the Latin American culture have caused some U.S.-based consultants to been ignored or fired because of their recommendations to replace family members who are not contributing to the business. The family believes they are staying true to the founder's values and the mission of the organization. For some family firms, adherence to long-term collective goals can be more valuable and fulfilling than profit.

Financial Performance

A recent area of research that has fueled considerable discussion and debate among scholars is the superior financial performance shown by larger family firms over their nonfamily counterparts. There is conflicting research on financial performance differences between family and nonfamily firms. Recent research has shown that family businesses show a higher return on investment,[17] have greater value, are operated more efficiently, and carry less debt compared to nonfamily businesses.[18] Jim Lee[19] showed that family firms in the Standard & Poor's 500 over the period 1992–2002 had higher profit margins and a higher reinvestment of revenues when compared with nonfamily firms. Anderson and Reeb[20] presented evidence showing that large family businesses in the Standard & Poor's 500 performed better than nonfamily firms did. Miller and Le Breton-Miller[21] wrote a book based on a yearlong study of 46 successful large family-controlled companies, including Hallmark, L. L. Bean, IKEA, the *New York Times*, SC Johnson, W. L. Gore, and Cargill. The authors showed evidence that family firms outperformed their nonfamily counterparts and presented key attributes of long-term, successful family firms. Family firms have been described as "nimbler, more customer oriented and quality focused, and more active in the community. As a result, they tend to outperform nonfamily firms."[22]

A study of 100 large family owned firms by Credit Suisse showed family firms have outperformed nonfamily firms by a wide margin on numerous financial measures for the ten year period 2006–2016 (CS Family 1000, 2017).

Members from the Boston Consulting Group studied 149 publicly traded, family controlled firms with sales of more than $1 billion. They compared results with a control group of nonfamily companies of the same size and sector, and country of origin. The results showed that during years of economic growth the family firms did not outperform their nonfamily peers. However, during times of recession the family owned firms significantly outperformed. When the researchers looked at data across numerous business cycles from 1997 to 2009, the average long term financial performance of the family firms was greater than for the nonfamily firms in every country studied. The researchers speculate this was due to several factors including, family firms focus more on resilience than performance. They do not maximize their profits during positive economic times to increase their survivability during bad times. They manage the downside more than they manage the upside. The family firms were very long term in their thinking, making decisions that would be beneficial 10–20 years later.[23]

Conversely, other research has presented the opposite view: that family firms are not efficient, do not manage their capital well, and have a lower return on investment. To help answer the question if family firms out-compete nonfamily firms, research was undertaken to find a definitive answer. The answer remains; it depends. One study looked at family business performance in a single industry and noted that an important variable is the specific industry the firm competes in should be considered.[24] Another study looked at 369 manufacturing businesses and found that family involvement in the management of the firm was a positive aspect and reduced its risk of failure.[25] A 2015 study examined more than 350 articles on family business from 37 finance and management journals and found family business performance was moderated by succession and proper and professional corporate governance.[26] No conclusive evidence for favoring the concept of family firm out-performance has been shown. The difference may lie in the conflicting definitions of what a family firm is. More research needs to be performed in this vitally important area. If the superior financial performance of family firms is found to be true, it could change many people's views of family businesses. The most important result may be a change in governmental policies to support and encourage family firms. Family business owners should be encouraged. They are doing some things right and actually may be doing them better than nonfamily firms.

Sources of Financial Capital

Debt

Family firms are famously debt averse. In a large nationwide study, 26% of surveyed firms reported no debt.[27] On the positive side, the aversion to debt may help family firms to be able to survive by having a readily available source of capital during a recession. On the negative side, the firm could be underleveraged and it might not be capitalizing on opportunities for growth. Family firms famously do not like bank debt or the conditions, the lack of privacy, and the accountability that come with it. Instead, they rely on self-funding, or patient capital, from family members and friends.

Conservatism and Risk

Family businesses often have a different perception of risk than nonfamily firms have. They see risk as high stakes, or to put it another way, the price of a bad decision is seen as too costly and thus can be interpreted as being too great a risk. Many family firms are financially conservative. Because the vast majority of the entire family's wealth is often tied up in the business itself, family decision makers are extremely reticent of putting the firm at risk of capital loss or, worse, insolvency. Family firms are not necessarily risk averse because being in business is a risk in itself. Instead, the family tries to minimize its risk as best as it can. When the risk has been reduced as much as possible, the family will then take steps to capitalize on an opportunity. The president of a $10 million agricultural, packaging, and distribution company described his attitude toward risk:

> You put some risk out there sometimes to feel the waters. Right now, with the poor economy, it's very little to no risk. When I'm feeling better, I might take a couple of more risks, when there's nothing much to risk. I can't risk much at this point. Me, personally, if I am at home and take a risk, it only affects me. But here, it affects others, like vendors I won't be paying. So I can't; I have to really watch the level of risk.[28]

The general manager of a $15 million general construction firm discussed risk: "We don't step into something we don't know. If we have an opportunity about something we do not know, about an area that's not in our area of expertise, we will pass on it."[29]

A family's conservative nature is often interpreted by outside stakeholders, such as suppliers, employees, and other professionals, as being nonprofessional and avoiding decisions, which is often a source of tension and frustration. Nothing could be farther from the truth. The preceding quote from the president of the agricultural firm is from the company that *created* an entirely new regional industry. The family took a huge risk in starting their entrepreneurial venture.

Growth

Some family businesses have made a conscious decision to embrace slow growth. Based on their desire for control and an unfavorable opinion of debt, the choice is to finance their own growth in a fiscally conservative manner. Many, in fact, of the majority of family firms can be described as small. Often a family firm can be described as a lifestyle firm, where the family identity is tied to the business, the family works the business, and they have no plans for growth. In this manner, they can be considered as self-employed. The corner grocery store that employs family members and some neighbors and has no plans for opening another store is an example.

An opposite point of view is provided by family *gazelles*, family firms that have grown amazingly fast.[30] The difference between slow-growth family firms and family gazelles is in their original mission, vision, and purpose. If the purpose of the firm is to seize opportunity and build wealth quickly without consideration of building a business to last for several generations, they embrace rapid growth strategies more readily.

Philanthropy and Community Service

Family businesses are significantly philanthropic and they give to the local community, educational institutions, religious charities, and international relief efforts. On average, family firms give a larger percentage of their profits than nonfamily firms. By far, the heaviest benefactor of the family's good intentions is the local community. Family firms are closely linked to their communities. Due to the usual small to medium size of most family businesses, these firms are often local or regional regarding their customers and employees. The values of the first generation of founders often emphasize involvement in the local community as a way to pay the community back for supporting their business over the years. Giving reinforces the family's values. Charitable giving is also a way for nonactive family members to be involved with the family and the business and to understand the relationship between business profits and giving. Many families take great pride in their philanthropic service and believe they are carrying on the legacy of the founder by doing so. Family business owners feel that doing philanthropy as a family had the benefit of bringing the family closer together.[31] The family receives more than just noneconomic benefits from their charitable giving. Family firms engaging in philanthropy were shown to have better performance.[32]

Often a family will decide to focus on certain issues, such as education, poverty, or entrepreneurship. This focus serves multiple functions: it enables the family to decide among numerous requests for funds, and it gives the family a broader influence and enables them to make a more visible difference by specifically targeting certain purposes. Often a family practices the social responsibility concept of "doing well by doing good," and they focus their giving on issues that are closely related to the firm's business. In this manner, the awareness of the family business is increased among its customers and community, as it is associated with the family giving and its support of a worthy purpose. The social status of the family is a motivational factor, as the family identity and respect within the community is valued, even among inactive family members.

SC Johnson has two charitable organizations: the SC Johnson Fund and the SC Johnson Foundation. The organization donates 5% of its pretax profits to charitable work, over twice that of the corporate average.[33]

With 143 companies and over 22,000 employees, the Philippines-based Lopez family has created the Lopez Group Foundation Inc. to oversee its 200-year-old family legacy of social responsibility, with charitable giving in education, poverty alleviation, and the environment.

Family Competitive Advantage in the Marketplace

Because the family's name and reputation is intertwined with the business, most family firms pursue a strategy of high quality at a fair price and provide excellent customer service. Customers of a family business reward the business by being loyal. The family has a long-term outlook, concern for stakeholders, and a good community standing. Mix these with the long-standing trust and loyalty the firm may have developed, and customers would rather do business with a family firm than with a faceless nonfamily corporate business. There is almost a sense of obligation from the firm's loyal customers and suppliers. Community members want to support responsible local businesses.

Family businesses should promote their family ownership and heritage, as it can be a source of tremendous competitive advantage regarding customers. Family businesses are seen by consumers as trustworthy, fair, and offering good value and excellent customer service. Customers believe if there is a problem, the family business is more likely to handle the situation in a satisfactory manner than a nonfamily or faceless corporate business would. In this age of empowered consumers and a "think locally" viewpoint, family firms should take advantage of one of their key strengths and heavily promote the differences with their nonfamily competitors. One family business that unabashedly promotes its familiness is SC Johnson, who adds the tagline "A family company" to their corporate identification and logo. Their corporate website details five generations of the Johnson family through the history of the company.

Because family firms utilize their own capital, they are able to make opportunistic investments without accountability to outsiders. Family firms are able to change direction quickly in a dynamic environment, giving the firm a significant competitive advantage, especially in a field where a first-mover advantage is vital. They often make intuitive or heuristic decisions that enable rapid decision making and provide the ability to seize opportunities.

Sharma and Irving[34] discussed the benefits of family social networks, including a ready source of easy-to-obtain, flexible, "patient" financial capital and family personnel who unite to improve the survivability of the business during tough times. Families who are most committed to the continuity of the family business have been shown to have three characteristics: (a) they believe owning the business helps fulfill the family mission, (b) they view the values exemplified by the business as a source of family pride, and (c) they believe they are contributing to the community and society in a meaningful way.[35]

The Squandered Advantage

The differences between a family firm and a nonfamily firm are numerous and account for a huge competitive advantage. However, for many family firms this can be a squandered advantage. We have already discussed trust is higher among the general public towards family firms, the quality and service is perceived to be better, that family firms listen to customers better, and that 66% would pay more. This is an incredible competitive advantage, however, it goes to waste if the family business does not advertise, promote, or let the public know they are *a family business*. Many family firm leaders fear embarrassment they will be thought of as small and unprofessional. Nothing could be farther than the truth. The research shows it and proves it. Customers, suppliers, and employees trust a family firm more than a nonfamily firm.[36] The sad fact is that only one out of every two customers knows which businesses they do business with are family firms.[37] This is a squandered competitive advantage. Almost one out of every three customers rely on social media to learn about a family business.

The opportunity is large, family owned businesses need to advertise the fact they are family owned, they need to discuss their family history, their family legacy and story, and they need to capitalize on the fact that consumers would rather pay more than a nonfamily competitor. The public believes quality and service is superior to nonfamily firms, so family owned firms should advertise their quality, their products and their unique differences. Lastly, and this may be an opportunity for the next generation, they business needs to tell these differences on social media. Social media is free, it just takes some knowledge (which the younger generation has), time, and a willingness to do so. The public desires it. Family firms should not squander the incredible competitive advantage they have in the minds of their consumers.

Guanxi

In Chinese family firms, there is a concept entitled Guanxi. The closest relationships are with one's own family, the next closest are extended family and close friend, the next level is with people who have similar shared experiences such as college classmates, the final level is with strangers who are often treated with suspicion until a relationship develops. Guanxi networks are invaluable in a country where the laws are not enforced equally. Guanxi networks are valuable trusted sources of information. For example, if a trusted family member recommends a business partner, it will be seen as a valuable recommendation. A foreigner with no relationships or history with the family or business, will have difficulty doing business until trust is developed. This is an incredible competitive advantage.[38]

The Resources of Successful Family Firms

A family has unique resources it can call on during startup or times of trouble. Five resources have been identified by studying successful family firms:

1. Human Capital in the form of very passionate and unusually motivated (an inexpensive) family employees.
2. Human Capital (2) in the form of unique knowledge gained only by mentorship and years in the business.
3. Social Capital in the form of trust and reputation. For example, when a daughter joins the family business her mother or father may pass down the high amount of trust and reputation they have built with customers, employees, and suppliers over many years. Family business social capital can be intergenerational.
4. Patient Financial Capital in the form of favorable terms and a low amount of "strings attached." It is much easier to get a loan from a member of one's own family than from a bank. The motivation to not take advantage of or disappoint a family member is strong. Financial stewardship is strong among family borrowers.
5. Risk Management, the last resource is important in terms of renewal of the family business during bad times and in entrepreneurial orientation. Family firms are superior to nonfamily firms in terms of

business longevity, however, many firms may cease to exist after the founding generation. These families may continue on in business together due to the ability to apply their unique reputational, financial, and knowledge capital in other ventures.[39, 40]

International Sales

In the previous edition of this book, it was discussed that the majority of family firms did not have significant if any international sales. This is not surprising considering their conservative nature, aversion to debt, avoidance of risk, and need for control. At the time, most US based family firms believed domestic competition was their biggest threat. That has recently changed. US based family firms have now embraced international trade and international operations as a way to escape entrenched low cost domestic competition. In a 2015 PWC survey of 154 U.S. based family firms, 60% had international sales.[41]

Family firms in smaller markets, such as European Union countries or in Latin America, have embraced international businesses as a way to diversify and break into new and larger markets. This may be an area for the succeeding generations to focus on as they enter their family firms. By gaining education or international business experience, they may add significant value when they join the family firm, which might lead them into new international business markets.

Spirituality and Religious Beliefs

A significant number of families in business together have strong religious beliefs and spiritual faith.[42] Their faith is an important element of who they are. It guides their value system and it affects how they do business. Based on their beliefs, their faith is exhibited in customer service and treating their customers and employees fairly. They embrace the stewardship and stakeholder approaches to family firms.

Chick-fil-A is a company whose owners have a strong faith. All locations are closed on Sundays due to their Christian beliefs. As discussed elsewhere in this book, those of the Muslim faith have strong beliefs concerning excessive profits. They do not charge interest, and their religion calls them to be philanthropic. Because of the family ownership and control of the business, they have more freedom to express their faith at their own place of business, compared with a nonfamily or corporate-owned firm.

Genogram

A tool that enables family members to better understand their family history and to recognize generational problematic issues is called the family genogram. The genogram is similar to a family tree, with the exception that it entails more detailed information than simply births and deaths. The genogram tracks branches of families; illnesses such as mental illness and alcoholism; genetic issues; marital status; and history, occupation, and critical incidents in the life of the family, such as tragic events or trauma. The genogram also can detail strong family messages through the generations, such as a family's desire to instill the need to work hard or the importance of gaining an education.

In my own family, my father instilled in me the importance of being self-employed and "my own man." I now pass this on to my children. Looking back, both of my grandfathers at one time or another were also self-employed. These types of family messages can be very powerful. Family therapists and consultants often advise families to create their genogram in order to understand and work through their issues more effectively. An example of a family genogram is in Figure 2.1.

The following are items of importance:

- Year of birth
- Year of death
- Relationships (marriage, living together, divorce, separation, broken relationship, adoption, close relationships or attachments among various family members)
- University graduates
- Occupations
- Entrepreneurial ventures and businesses

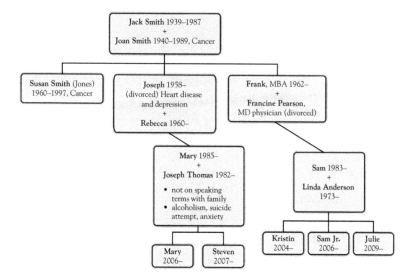

Figure 2.1. Genogram for ABC Machine Tool Co. The Smith family.

As shown in the Smith family genogram, there are some important issues for the family to be aware of in the form of divorces, family conflict, cancer, heart disease, alcoholism, and mental illness.

CHAPTER 3

Family Business Theories

Life Cycles of a Family Business

There are several different life cycles (or stages) families need to consider concerning family firms. A usual life cycle model, such as one that marketing professionals use to plan and manage new products, describes the four stages of birth, growth, maturity, and decline. Family firms go through similar stages as individuals, as a family, and as an organization. Individuals advance through several standard life cycle stages: preadulthood (birth through age 15), provisional adulthood (16–30), early adulthood (31–45), middle adulthood (46–60), late adulthood (61–75), and late-late adulthood (75-plus years).

Each member of the family passes through his or her individual life cycle at varying times. As a result, the family life cycle does not have the same standard sequence the individual life cycle does, with its pattern of birth through death. The family life cycle is more variable. It needs to be thought of as a system, with various family members at differing individual stages entering and leaving the firm. Marriages, divorces, retirement, and children increase the complexity of the family business system.

The organizational life cycle stages usually follow the standard life cycle model of birth, growth, maturity, and decline (death). However, an organization, unlike individuals or family members, can live forever. Over the history of the firm, there may be periods of rapid dynamic growth and change followed by periods of slow growth. The family should prevent atrophy by staying alert to opportunities.

To add more layers of complexity in the business, each of the firm's products has its own product life cycle, the industry itself has a life cycle, and the economy of the nation or the world has a life cycle of expansion or contraction. For the family business to prosper, owners and managers should evaluate their stages and apply the appropriate strategies to recognize their opportunities or limit their risk. There can be significant turmoil among the various cycles as new members enter the family firm, as the business environment contracts or expands, and as company leadership retires and exits the firm.

Figure 3.1 depicts the generational life cycle of a family business as it moves through successions from one generation to another. As you can see, the successions between the generations are not separate, with a clean break between generations. Instead, there is often a time when the next generation comes into power while the exiting generation is slowly reducing power.

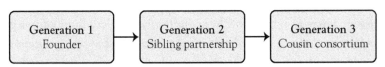

Figure 3.1. Generational succession of family firms.

Source: Adapted from Gersick et al. (1997).

The Systems Approach

Tagiuri and Davis[1] created the three-circle model of the family business (see Figure 3.2), which has become the primary conceptual model for family business studies. The model presents family business as consisting of three complex and overlapping subsystems of ownership, family, and business. The model has been instrumental in understanding many of the complexities and dynamics within the family business domain.

The intersections where the three circles meet explain the possible competitive advantages of family firms, as well as the disadvantages. With the three subsystems in mind, it is easy to understand the differences between family members who are in different subsystems. For instance, a family member who is an owner but not an employee (resides in two circles), may be more inclined to consider a buyout offer than a family member who is both an owner and a member of management (resides in all three circles). The entrepreneurial founder, who may have full ownership and control (resides in three circles), may not be willing to pay high salaries to employees who are family members but not owners of the firm (two circles). A family member who resides in only one circle (as a

Family

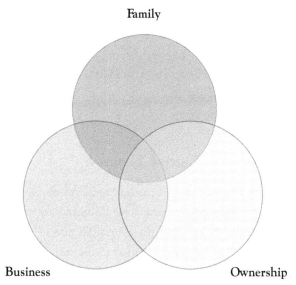

Business   Ownership

Figure 3.2. The three-circle model.

Source: Adapted from Tagiuri and Davis (1996).

nonowner and nonemployee) will have a different viewpoint, concerns, and goals than one who resides in two or in all three circles.

Where the family and business systems overlap, situations can become ripe for disagreement. The family system requires closeness and harmony with a lack of conflict, while the business system needs change and healthy conflict in order to grow, prosper, and to make good business decisions. The family members (depending on whether they are active or inactive) may have differing goals, and

ownership structure aside, what differentiates family business from management-controlled businesses are often the intentions, values, and strategy-influencing interactions of owners who are members of the same family. The result is a unique blending of family-management-ownership interaction subsystems that can produce an entire family business system. This family-management-ownership interaction can produce significant adaptive capacity and competitive advantage. Alternatively, it can be the source of significant vulnerability in the face of generational or competitive change.[2]

A new model was created detailing the interactions of family, business, and management, which is referred to as the unified systems perspective. Instead of three interrelated and overlapping circles, the unified systems theory shows that the family, business, individuals, and their actions and outcomes as one interrelated continuous circle.[3] This shows that all elements are equally important.

Agency Theory

The idea that a nonfamily member would not have the same incentive, motivation, and diligence as an owner would have and would possibly engage in self-serving behavior is the central feature of agency theory. To prevent this potential conflict of interest, the owner installs managers and provides them with controls, procedures, and policies to limit the effect of this conflict of interest, thus creating agency costs. Many experts believe that family businesses have fewer agency costs because of the shared ownership and management functions.

Family business scholars put forward agency theory to explain the competitive advantage held by many family firms. However, while agency theory highlights positive benefits, it can also be a reason behind poorly performing family businesses due to unprofessional management, entrenched leadership, and altruistic behavior. There can be both negative and positive agency benefits within the family firm.

The Resource-Based Approach

It is believed that the resource-based view of the firm (RBV) may explain the competitive advantage of many family firms over nonfamily firms.[4] The RBV states that a family firm has a set of unique capabilities, resources, and relationships that nonfamily firms do not have and cannot develop. Five sources of family firm capital may help to explain the positive effects from the RBV theory: human capital, social capital, patient capital, survivability, and governance structures. The advantage for a family firm stems from the interaction of the family and the business in the unique way that they manage, evaluate, acquire, discard, bundle, and leverage their resources.[5]

The term "familiness" has been used to describe the unique and differing aspects of a family business when compared with nonfamily businesses. The term describes the interplay between the family and the business, including a social aspect that affects the strategic decisions of the business.[6]

The Stewardship Approach

In the stewardship perspective of family firms, the family behaves and acts as caretakers of the firm. The family feels it is their responsibility to oversee the firm in a responsible manner, which respects the generations who came before, and to pass the firm on to the next generation successfully. Stewards place knowledgeable professionals on the board who can give objective advice. The board members are chosen to complement the skills (or lack thereof) of the family. Examples of this perspective are the larger Standard & Poor's 500 family-controlled firms who have a strong board of directors entrusted to give objective counsel. Most all of these types of companies are managed with outside professionals, such as Ford and Wal-Mart. Research has shown that improved decision making occurs in family firms with strong, active boards.[7]

Socioemotional Wealth (SEW)

Since the first edition of this book was published, another theory of family business has come into strong favor. Socioemotional Wealth (SEW). This theory makes a very strong argument that helps to explain the altruistic nature of families in business. To the family there are often things of greater importance than mere financial rewards. The family places great value on the social and emotional aspects of participation with the family business. The family may have a strong emotional tie to their business and will want to keep the dynasty preserved. The family social status may be dependent upon the family business. To sell the firm would harm the family social status in the community, reducing their social capital.[8] For example, a 100 year old private firm that receives a very lucrative buyout offer which values the company at several times its real worth, may decline the offer due to the important role the business plays in the family's identify and values. They may say no because they want to keep the family dynasty alive and preserve the legacy of the founder and the family. This research has been discussed as possibly being the dominant paradigm in family business research.[9]

Stakeholder Theory

The stakeholder theory fell out of favor compared with other theories of management. Recently, it has generated renewed interest among family business researchers, as it entails all the key stakeholders of a family firm. Stakeholders can be described as any people who have an interest in or can be affected by the firm. This includes shareholders, employees, the community, other family members, suppliers, and customers. Stakeholder theory is able to assimilate and provide justification for the altruistic nature of many family businesses.[10]

CHAPTER 4

Family Business Decision Making

How Families in Business Make Decisions

Although it is of vital importance to a family firm, there is little information on the subject of family business decision making. The most useful information is contained in a single article from Aronoff and Astrachan,[1] who found that 34% of founders made the decisions themselves, 48% of family businesses searched for a consensus, and 6% discussed the issue and took a vote. Fifty-three percent of the voting group is made up of the third generation of family leadership. This suggests a higher level of governance and professionalism among the later generations, accounting for better planning and organizational control.[2] An increased use of succession planning among both the second and third generations also gives evidence of a higher degree of professionalism in later generation family firms.[3]

The research shows conflicting data in our existing knowledge of family business decision making. Feltham, Feltham, and Barnett[4] discussed the situation of a single, dominant, key decision maker; Aronoff and Astrachan[5] discussed a single decision maker in the majority of firms they studied but found a large number of firms searching for consensus and some firms using a democratic voting process. Family values, personality traits, and their fit within the firm were found to be more influential than strict professionalism in a study of human resources decision making.[6]

Ibrahim, Angelides, and Parsa[7] discovered a nimbler and faster decision-making process compared with nonfamily firms. Conversely, Prince and File[8] described a slower decision-making process, with more people involved, and Miller and Le Breton-Miller[9] recorded decisions based on the beliefs and values of the family. Miller and Le Breton-Miller[10] discussed how Francois Michelin, the former CEO of Michelin, made decisions. When faced with "tough decisions," he did not make decisions by the financials or the investment community "but according to the enduring beliefs of the family."[11]

Prince and File[12] conducted several significant research studies on marketing to family businesses from the financial services perspective, including a 1995 study that presented the problems and issues associated with selling products to family businesses. These issues included

- multiple decision makers
- decision makers not actively involved in the business
- a significantly longer decision-making time requiring multiple calls and meetings

File[13] surveyed the decisions of 396 family businesses involving both significant family involvement and a lack of family involvement. File divided the family business decisions into four groups:

- *Category 1.* The decisions had high importance to the business and evoked significant family involvement. These decisions included compensation, benefits, and financial allocation and capital equipment decisions. Included were consulting services decisions and marketing communication decisions.
- *Category 2.* The decisions had a high importance to the business but evoked little or no family involvement. These decisions included technically complex purchases such as accounting services, property insurance, legal services, software purchases, computer equipment, security services, and telephone leases and purchases.
- *Category 3.* The decisions had a low importance to the business but evoked significant family involvement. Decisions included employee insurance, buy-sell agreements, and highly visible corporate philanthropy efforts.
- *Category 4.* The decisions had low importance to the business and evoked little or no family involvement. Decisions included travel agency decisions, car leasing, office design, long-distance providers, and printing services.

An important finding in File's[14] work was the increased involvement of the family in issues that could include favorable exposure of the family and its business philosophy to the community, such as marketing communications and philanthropic efforts. Confirming File's work on family involvement and delays in decision making, Sharma and Manikutty[15] reported that increased family involvement, increased divestment decision making, and resource evaluation decision times.

Goffe and Scase[16] highlighted controlling family members and a lack of delegation to nonfamily management employees on key decisions as important elements in family businesses. They studied delegated decision making in 12 family firms in the general building and personal services sectors in the United Kingdom. Four of the firms were operated by the first-generation founder, while the remaining eight were inherited. The firms ranged in size from 30 employees to 1,200 employees, with an average employee count of 300. They found a fluid type of decision making characterized by a lack of management formalization. Family member owners used a consultative approach with management, yet it was the owners who made the important decisions. When the authority was given to make decisions at a lower level, management was "allowed to make some of the decisions some of the time."[17] They showed that, even when delegating, ownership retained control of decision making through the use of "insidious controls, setting of agendas, strict regulation of the amount of information available, and communication channels."[18] Positions that required "overall control"[19] were reserved for family members.

Carney found the attributes of family firms that result in their ability to outperform nonfamily firms are "embedded"[20] in the firm's system of corporate governance. Based on the nature of ownership and control "rights,"[21] family firms exercised the rights in decision making on a level that is not available to those in nonfamily governance systems. According to Poza, "Family businesses may be able to make decisions more quickly and therefore take advantage of opportunities that others may miss. Quick decision making is critical in business, and tight-knit families in business move fast."[22]

In a study of over 300 family executives, family firms had quicker and more effective decision making because they had less bureaucracy. The decision-making hierarchy "may be completely ignored, existing only to be bypassed,"[23] which often frustrates outsiders. People who are accustomed to working in corporate environments consider so much overlap of job responsibilities and the lack of clearly defined roles and responsibilities to be messy and confusing. This may help to explain the negative connotation of family firms being unprofessional mom & pops that lack management skills. Often, when a family business makes a personnel decision, they use the perspective of family values and personality fit issues, rather than basing decisions on strict performance criteria.[24]

A Model of Second-Generation Family Business Decision Making

To fully understand the nature of family business decision making, the differences between the generations should be explored. An entrepreneur is often a dominant personality who makes most of the decisions. This leaves succeeding generations ill prepared for decision making in the absence of the founder. Heavy dependence on a single entrepreneurial founder underscores the centralized decision-making process common in the vast majority of first-generation firms. In a study of 765 family firm executives, the organization was either dependent or very dependent on a single decision maker in 75% of the firms surveyed. Feltham et al. discovered founders exhibit such control over decision making that 31% made all the major decisions, including 87% of all finance decisions. Entrepreneurial founders also tended to utilize intuition and heuristics as a way to make decisions.[25]

Research among 15 senior-level second-generation family business members (depicted in Figure 4.1) showed the second generation did not make decisions without complete information unless forced, did not feel comfortable utilizing intuition, engaged in a broad search for knowledge and more information, and had a larger social network they used to gather information and discuss business issues than their first-generation predecessors did. The second generation used a consultative decision-making style to obtain the needed information and arrive at a decision. These are major areas of difference, compared with the first generation. The second generation therefore seems more rational than the previous generation, yet not as rational as the third generation. The third generation is different from the second generation with a tendency toward the more professional consensus approach and majority voting.

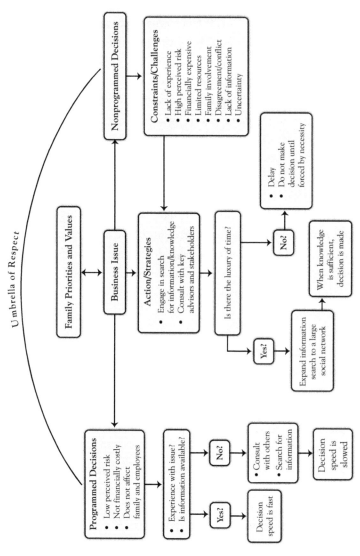

Figure 4.1. A model of second-generation family business decision making.

Source: Alderson (2009).

The need and ability for family decision makers to obtain whatever information is required is exemplified as follows:

> I make my decisions the reverse of my parents. When I make decisions that I have the authority to make, I'll talk to one of the managers who it will affect. I'll talk to my parents about it, talk to who it concerns, talk about the issues, and then I'll make the decision.[26]
>
> I mine for more information. Always, if I don't feel I have enough information to make the decision, I'll do whatever is necessary to make the decision. I'll do whatever is necessary to get more information. One thing I want . . . you know . . . haste just causes more mistakes in the long run.[27]

Figure 4.1 shows the umbrella of respect at the top of the model, overseeing all the activities of the firm. This term describes the high level of respect and reverence for the accomplishments of the first generation. All decisions are immediately filtered through the founders' stated priorities and values. The decision maker first makes sure the decision is not in conflict with the family's mission. Then, the decision maker proceeds to make the decision.

All decisions are divided into two main types: programmed decisions (i.e., small decisions or those made numerous times before) and nonprogrammed decisions (i.e., larger decisions that are made infrequently). These decisions almost always lack adequate information to make a good decision. They are financially costly, perceived as risky, and often involve several other members of the family. The result is a slowed decision-making process.

A retail store owner discussed the respect he has for his father's accomplishments:

> Dad ran a very successful large corporation (*Fortune* 500). He retired and went out on top. He started this company in 1982. I learned all I know from him. I am not real bright; Dad is, though. I always yield to him. I have a lot of respect for Dad. I am lucky; he's like a prop. I am not sure what I am going to do when he dies.[28]

A third-generation retail store owner described his father, only half jokingly:

> Now that he's gone, I look back and he was right. It's like Samuel Clemmons said: When you're 5 years of age, Dad is great; at 15, he's a moron; and later in life, Dad was pretty smart! My dad was like God. No, he advised God! He was God's advisor![29]

The Family Business Rationality Continuum seen in Figure 4.2 graphically depicts the increase in rationality from the first through the third generations. There is no data specifically focusing on the fourth generation and their decision-making processes. Based on the larger family size and business growth, it is likely that the fourth generation is increasingly rational as well, including embracing the addition of nonfamily professional management.

The third generation is often larger than the second generation. It involves various family members, many of them equal partners, including some family members who may not be employed at the family business

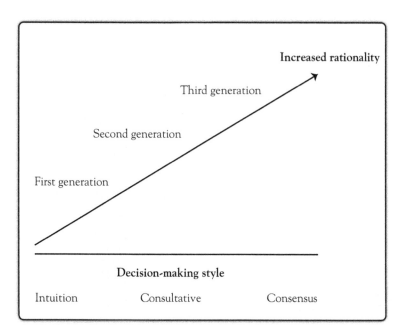

Figure 4.2. Family business rationality continuum.

Source: Alderson (2009).

but who have an ownership stake. To maintain harmony, family members often use a consensus style of decision making and often a majority vote is taken. This increase in rationality was confirmed in the literature by Aronoff and Astrachan,[30] who determined the third generation (the cousin consortium) used the more rational consensus or voting approach.

Research has shown the longer a family firm has been established, the more successful the firm is. Especially if a generational transfer has occurred, rationality and logical decision making increases. In other words, family members make decisions more carefully, with a variety of solicited inputs, in order to maximize the decision effectiveness.

CHAPTER 5

Family Business Issues and Generational Differences

Nepotism

Nepotism refers to the process of hiring or promoting employees simply because they are family members. A commonly heard derisive comment when discussing junior family members is, "They have the right last name." Family firms can have the view that all family members deserve jobs, regardless of qualifications. Often, this leads to too many unqualified, unproductive employees. Free-riding family members can lead to poor morale among the nonfamily employees. The forced hiring of an undeserving or ineffective family member because of pressure from other more powerful family members is a common cause of significant family conflict as well. It is also an underlying reason that key nonfamily management leave the family firm. Those who leave cite frustration and a lack of promotional opportunities for advancement.

The president of a $2.5 million third-generation personal services company described being forced by his parents to employ his sister. He described the difficulty of the issue of family employment:

My sister lost her job. I felt obligated to hire her, had to hire her. Parents wanted me to. I went against my will and let her work here. It was awful. She was making up lies about me and my dad. It finally came to a head and I had to get rid of her. That was a big decision, because now I'm the [expletive]. My parents were not happy about it. It's the best thing I ever did. She had no respect for me or my father. If you don't respect someone, how can they work for you? I still pay for her gas, though.[1]

Communication

One of the main issues for family business can be a lack of communication among family members. Effective, open communication among all family members, including the various generations, is critical. This is a critical core competency that needs to exist for the firm to develop and succeed. In studies of successful and long-lasting family-owned firms, healthy communication was found to be one of the main components of their success; it is "indispensible."[2] Without effective communication among the participants, the business will most likely fail to succeed to the next generation.

In most families, communication is not perfect, but in a family business there must be a sincere and significant effort to communicate to others who are stakeholders in the business. Many families have found it beneficial to have family meetings and institute a family council in order to make sure all family members are "in the loop" concerning important decisions, opportunities, expenditures, and in order to give everyone a voice.

Compensation

Compensation for family members in small family firms is often higher than nonfamily members receive and higher than comparable outside positions. This can lead to family member dependence on the firm, as they become accustomed to the high standard of living. It becomes a two-edged sword, as the family member often feels trapped by a lack of alternative employment choices with a similar level of compensation. More professionally managed family firms have compensation policies to decide pay grades, salaries, and ranges for each position, whether family or nonfamily. The pay grades should be comparable with comparable firms. Compensation for work performed (employment) is different than ownership dividends. A firm may elect to give owners of the firm a bonus, or dividend distribution.

Conflict

Starting with the sibling rivalry between Cain and Abel, there has been dysfunction and conflict within families. One of the first published articles on family business was on the subject of family conflict, proposing that family conflict is commonplace and inevitable.[3] Since that time, the awareness of conflict and the seriousness of the issues has increased significantly. This has resulted in the creation and use of many techniques, tools, and procedures to better manage the conflict by attempting to reduce its negative impact or prevent it altogether. Family therapists and family business consultants have sprung up to provide conflict management services to family firms.

When the family system, with its often petty and frivolous but deep-seated resentments, emotions, interpersonal conflicts, rivalries, mistrust, favoritism, and nepotism, is combined with the business system in which family members' roles, employment, identity, and financial wealth are intertwined, problems can explode in size.[4] The potential for conflict can grow exponentially with the age and growth of the business and with increased numbers of family participants. By the third generation, there are typically several grandchildren working in the business. Often they are cousins, who may have a variety of goals and objectives.

Family businesses can be rife with dysfunction and conflict. An extreme example of the perils of family business conflict is the Italian leather goods producer Gucci. When the family patriarch, Guccio Gucci, died in 1953, the children and grandchildren began bitter and expensive legal battles, which finally resulted in blackmail and murder.

Ford Motor Company founder Henry Ford installed his son, Edsel, as president and then constantly second-guessed and undercut him. Browbeaten and exhausted, Edsel died at age 49. Edsel's mother, wife, and children believed Henry was responsible for Edsel's early death.

Napa Valley winemaking pioneer Robert Mondavi was fired by his mother from the family business after a fistfight with his younger brother. He immediately started his own family winery and became a competitor to the family business and eventually was more successful.

The Dart Group, which owned Crown Books, went through the divorce of the founders and the firing of the founder of Crown Books,

Robert M. Half, by his father, Howard H. Half. Years of litigation resulted. The firm eventually went bankrupt and was sold.

The Ambani brothers of Reliance Industries, one of India's largest companies, had a highly public struggle for control of the conglomerate after the death of their father. After much acrimony and endless legal battles, the company was split in half, with the petroleum and petrochemicals business going to one brother, and the telecom, financial services, and electricity business going to the other. The dispute went on for years until it was finally mediated by professional advisors with pressure from their mother.

In 2002, 19-year-old Liesel Pritzker (Marmon Group, Hyatt Hotels) sued her father and 11 older cousins to prevent them from misusing her and her brother's trust funds. The family businesses conglomerate, which was developed over 100 years, was to be liquidated and split among the heirs.

The winemaking family of Ernest and Julio Gallo has entered its third generation. However, the brothers were accused of locking their younger brother Joseph out of the family business. When Joseph found success as a cheese producer, his older brothers sued to bar him from using the Gallo brand name on his products.

The reason we have Adidas and Puma athletic shoes is due to a conflict between the Dassler brothers. One brother left and started the competing brand.

The conflict in the early 1900s between Alfred I. du Pont and his cousin, Pierre du Pont, over who would control their family chemical company was so contentious that Alfred built a stone wall around his property, topped it with shards of glass, and told his relatives to stay out. They also bought competing newspapers in the same town and waged war in the marketplace.

Familial conflict and bickering are associated with the poor succession rate in family businesses. Due to this conflict, the second and third generations may decide to leave the family firm. Often they are overwhelmed with guilt at the prospect of leaving the family business and feel as if they would be abandoning their family. Yet if they stay, many become bitter and contribute to infighting and a lack of productivity. Conversely, in their desire for harmony, many family businesses squelch any differences of opinion and thus stifle healthy debate. It is difficult for sons and daughters to disagree with their father or mother because such action is quickly seen as disloyal and disruptive. Such lack of open communication has the effect of limiting not only potential business options but also the entire strategic planning process. The result is often a forced dependence on the status quo, resulting in reduced market share, lack of investment in new and emergent businesses areas, and failure to recognize competitive threats on the horizon, accompanied by product stagnation and business decline.

Conflict has both positive and negative elements, and families must strike a fine balance between too much conflict and not enough. Three main types of conflict appear in family businesses: task conflict, process conflict, and relationship conflict. Task conflict is associated with goals, strategies, and the discussion of opposing strategic paths. Process conflict is associated with how work should be accomplished, the appropriate use of personnel, and how much responsibility each person should have. When these two types of conflict are present in moderation within an organization, better decisions result.

Conflict is usually expressed in communication and behavioral problems. Simple conflicts can be resolved easily and do not impede effective decision making. Common sense and reason will usually prevail. Complex conflicts are heavy with emotion, commonly resulting in lack of productivity and the failure to make decisions. This type of conflict is very often chronic and it makes its presence known as it comes and goes within a company. The remedy for complex conflict is to enlist outside professional resources. Therapists or family counselors, as well as organizational behavioral experts, can help a family work through the complex issues of serious conflict. The most negative form of conflict is relationship conflict, which is the type of conflict most often seen in family business. Relationship conflict is characterized by anger, hostility, resentment, and worry, which can result in a complete lack of productivity.

Conflict has a profusion of negative effects on the family and the business, and it is a huge disruption to effective decision making. It can lead to poor decision making or lack of decision-making ability. Irrational decision making can become rampant, and decisions may be made on an emotional rather than a logical and rational basis. Often there is no proper acceptance or buy-in about decisions from the dissenting family members. When a family-owned company cannot make decisions, it is not hard to see the effect on employees, the business, and its customers. It is a no-win situation when family members are in competition with each other. When conflict is resolved, fast decisions can take place, and most importantly, better decisions can be made from the open discussion and debate over alternate possibilities.

Family firms sometimes find themselves in a situation where the needs of the family's lifestyle are so great that they take precedence over the needs of the firm, or the family cannot decide on the firm's strategic direction and the management of the business. The result can be a sale of the family assets or a slow decline in the business, as financial resources are drained away, decisions are not made, and competitors eventually overwhelm the firm. The result is usually an end to the family business.

Families and their consultants should be vigilant to the negative and destructive impact of conflict on the effective management of the firm and the healthy functioning of the family. Once conflict is identified, it is best dealt with family counseling or intervention at an early stage. A common practice among many families is to ignore the conflict and not talk about it. This avoidance strategy is short term. The conflict wil l eventually come out and it will be harder and more problematic to deal with when it does. Rarely, family businesses devolve into such unhealthy situations that neither family business consultants nor family therapists can help. Many times this is due to a lack of emotional development on the part of the parents and the children's anxiety, stemming from a desire to both please and break away from their parents. In this type of negative situation, the children should explore other opportunities for employment outside the family business because being in business together is not a healthy or positive situation for any of the members.

A study of 1,454 top managers in small and midsized family businesses found that 34% had argued about the future direction of the company and 27% had argued about the contribution of other employed family members. Twenty percent experienced tension over roles of in-laws, over who was and was not allowed to work in the business, and over a lack of consultation on key decisions with other family members.[5] In a study of 15 long-lived firms, 93% of the conflict was found to be between siblings and rarely if ever between the generations. In almost all the cases, the conflict was over the roles of family employees.[6]

On a positive note, many family members do not report the presence of significant conflict in their business. They commonly disagree about certain issues, and they agree that disagreements happen almost daily. However, they do not experience the kind of interpersonal, destructive conflict described earlier. A retail store owner, speaking about his father, the founder of a retail chain, said, "Most of the time when we disagreed, he was right, in the end."[7] The president of a third-generation family retailer said, "Not that we never disagreed, but we never dwelt on it."[8]

Lack of Planning

There is an old adage that says, "Failure to plan is planning to fail." The vast majority of family businesses do fail to plan effectively; only 37% of surveyed firms had a strategic plan.[9] This not only shows a tremendous opportunity for family businesses to improve their performance but also illuminates a need for more effective decision making. Family businesses that have a strategic plan also usually have board meetings, written hiring policies, buy-sell agreements, a formal valuation of company worth, more employees, and are more likely to have selected the successor. More importantly, they have higher sales and higher international sales as well.[10] These positive outcomes point to the importance of the strategic plan in helping the company manage the business in a more rational and professional manner that can boost performance and effectiveness.

In a survey of family business owners by the giant accounting firm KMPG, the following issues and challenges were rated as most troublesome or important:[11]

1. Growing profitably
2. Balancing different interests
3. Dealing with regulatory challenges
4. Planning succession
5. Determining future directions
6. Exiting by retirement
7. Establishing professional business management
8. Selling the business
9. Managing family relationships
10. Addressing international growth

Differences Among the Generations

Generation 1: Founder and Entrepreneur

During the start-up phase of the business, the founder-entrepreneur has sole decision-making ability. Entrepreneurs are generally individuals who like to create and have control. They are self-made risk takers who often have their personal identity tied up with their business, and they may feel that the business is their "baby." The founder has enjoyed success and is accustomed to being a one-man show. The leadership style of this owner-manager is often a transactional my-way-or-the-highway style, sometimes with a paternalistic style of management. The founders are usually quite private and do not share inner workings of their firm with people outside the firm. They are also very debt averse and have a strong need for control.

A common issue among future generations in a business is the continuing influence of the founder, who towers above the entire organization, a phenomenon referred to as "founder centrality"[12] or "generational shadow."[13] Such influence can have both positive and negative factors associated with it. It helps future generations in that they tend to follow the original mission or vision of the organization as set by the founder, including the importance of caring for long-term employees, the community, and their customers. The president of a $10 million retail dealership spoke about an employee who was kept on during poor economic times: "She is like family; she was here when my mother started the firm."[14] A second-generation owner of a retail gift store with annual revenue over $1 million explained,

> My priorities are honesty and fairness: basic values. It comes back to my father: integrity, honesty, simple ideas like that. It's the core character of who we are. My dad got this from his dad. Is it good for the people? Money will come if we treat people with respect and give fantastic customer service. They will be happy and loyal.[15]

The influence becomes negative if the successive generations are not allowed to make their own decisions or are second-guessed by the meddling founders who have not fully retired. This negative influence has been a major reason for succeeding generational members to exit the family firm.

In a study of 15 long-term, second-generation family firms, the positive contributions associated with the founders were many and they were readily apparent. Instead of a negative shadow, there was a reverence and awe for the previous generation's accomplishments. The term *umbrella of respect* was created to describe this phenomenon.[16]

In the second-generation firms, parental influence permeated all the decisions and activities of the family business in a guiding and positive manner. Often, decisions were made intentionally to enhance the parents' legacy and to make them proud, not to embarrass them. Decisions were often made based on what the parents would have done when faced with a similar situation. The high level of reverence the second generation had for the first generation was partly responsible for the tendency of the second generation to make decisions based on the values and mission of the family business. The founders contributed in a positive manner years after their retirement from the business, by establishing the family values and business mission used by the second generation to make business decisions. Here is the president of a $15 million agricultural firm, speaking about his parents:

They're always behind every decision I make, in that we make the decisions how they would want us to make the decisions. We ask ourselves, "What would Mom and Dad do?" They're such wonderful people. They don't want to screw anyone. They want everybody to get along; very neat people. He's definitely not the typical, "I built this before you were in diapers, and it's my baby." I don't get that attitude from them. My parents are, "You're the man!" I know if they died tomorrow, they know I love them and they love me. It's wonderful, a great relationship. I want that man to be so proud of the work we've done here. I want my mom to be idealized by everybody. That, in itself, is the ultimate goal for me. They are going out in style. They're hugely respected by the community, and respected and idealized by their friends.[17]

Generation 2: Sibling Partnership

In time, the second generation becomes involved in the business, consisting of the founder's sons and daughters and, often, their spouses. The second generation, usually involving a partnership of siblings, has been referred to as "the crucial generation" for the future success of the family firm.[18] Gersick et al. discussed the ability of the second generation to make decisions as a "critical capacity"[19] for the continued success of the firm. In a second-generation firm, the first generation (if not retired or deceased) may still be actively working and involved. This situation creates an interesting dynamic, as the two generations learn to work and manage together as they progress through their life cycles.

Generation 3: The Cousin Consortium

Problems are compounded and become more complex when the larger third generation is involved. The larger the family is, the greater is the possibility of separate motives and agendas, disagreements, and conflicts. This generation is referred to as a cousin company or cousin consortium. Made up of the grandchildren of the original founders—that is, the sons and daughters of the second-generation siblings—there may be numerous cousins. For example, consider a sibling partnership made up of two brothers and a sister, each of them having three children. Now, there may be as many as nine cousins involved in the family business, with each one having equal ownership rights. The management of the family firm under a cousin consortium like this can often be overwhelming. The family business needs to implement proper governance tools, such as creating a family constitution and initiating a family council with a majority vote.

CHAPTER 6

Succession

The ability to carry on a successful intergenerational transfer of owner-ship and leadership (succession) is by far the single most important family business issue. It is also the most researched topic in the area of family business. Most family businesses do not have a successful transition of ownership from the founding generation to the second generation. Stud-ies have generally agreed that approximately 30% of businesses transfer to the second generation, while only 10%–15% successfully transfer from the second generation to the third generation.[1] Only 4% manage to stay in the same family in the fourth generation.[2]

The majority of family firms want to keep the business in the fam-ily and pass it on to the next generation. The American Family Business Survey (2002) found that 85% of the firms surveyed wanted to continue with family ownership.[3] The Laird Norton Tyee Family Business Survey[4] found that 55% of the senior generation wanted successive generations to take over and almost 85% of the family businesses that had chosen a successor selected a family member to carry on the business. Succession has often been called the final act of greatness. How ideal for a family business founder to have his creation live on long after he or she is gone: That is a legacy.

One survey reported 77% of failed family businesses that declared bankruptcy did so after the death of the founder.[5] A family-owned business is more likely to fail due to lack of a succession plan upon the founder's illness or death than for reasons having to do with competition or market forces. Many family business researchers agree that the primary underlying reasons for failed successions are a lack of effective decision making and a lack of proper planning. Often this decision *not to plan* is caused by an owner who cannot concede power or will not tolerate a reduction in personal authority, responsibilities, or control.

The reasons for this scenario are numerous and can be quite complicated from a psychological perspective. Often, the previous generation simply does not want to be put out to pasture. Especially if they are the founders of the business, they often feel the company is their *baby* and their identity is closely interrelated with the company. Others equate retirement with death and simply do not want to discuss the issue. Of the CEO respondents to a large nationwide study, 13.4% reported they would never retire.[6] This causes much consternation in the family, especially the next generation members. The next generation waiting in the wings wonders when they will ever get their chance to lead.

Awareness of the life cycle stages becomes apparent when first initiating conversations regarding succession. Research has shown that at certain ages, the relationship of the founder and the successor can be either rife with conflict or relatively smooth. This is especially relevant in a father-to-son generational transfer. When a founder is in his relatively young 40s and 50s, and the successor is in his 20s or early 30s, the role conflict can be at its worst—and most visible. The current familial roles of each family member in their respective life cycles present barriers to effective communication and to efficient working relationships. Conversely, if a founder is in his 60s or 70s and the successor is in his 40s, the competition and conflict is less, producing a more positive working relationship.

An interesting discussion concerns the fact that many business researchers describe succession as the sole measurement of family business success. If a family business did not have a successful succession to the next generation, it would be considered a failure. However, if the goal of the firm was to work with family and build wealth, and they decided to capture the value of the business through an outright sale, why should that be considered a failure of the family firm?

Families have many reasons for not passing on the family business to future generations. Some of them are not necessarily negative, such as the case with the creation of significant family wealth. The children or grandchildren may have been brought up with a very high standard of living: they may have been educated at prestigious universities and they might prefer a professional vocation such as law or medicine. They might also have interests in benefitting society, such as working or volunteering at a nonprofit organization instead of working in the family business. This type of situation should not be considered a failure. Does the company still exist? Are its products still available to the public? If so, then the company was, and still is, a success.

In a study of children from family firms in their first year of college, 20% wanted to be working at the family business within 5 years, 38% were planning to return to the firm "sometime," and 42% said never. It is interesting to note that 70% of these respondents scored the firm *high* or *very high* for authoritarian management practices.[7]

The media is filled with stories of wealthy third-generation members who make headlines from their outrageous behavior and spendthrift patterns. Based on the fact that few family firms have a successful ownership transition to future generations, there is a well-known adage that states, "shirtsleeves to shirtsleeves in three generations." It refers to the first-generation entrepreneur who starts out poor, works very hard, and becomes tremendously successful. The second generation watched their parents work hard and suffer for the business, and most often, the second generation worked right alongside their parents. By the time the second generation had their children, the wealth was building as the family business achieved success. Unfortunately, the third-generation children were often brought up with a sense of entitlement, became spoiled, engaged in out-of-control spending, had a low work ethic, and eventually lost the business. The adage has some universal truth to it, as many countries have their own versions:

- In Italy, it is stated this way: "Barn stalls, to the stars, to the barn stalls in three generations."
- In Portugal, the first generation is *pay rice* (a rich farmer), the second generation is *filch noble* (a noble son), and the third generation is *net pore* (a poor grandson).
- In Mexico, it is "father/entrepreneur, son/playboy, grandson/ beggar."
- In China, the saying is "The first generation builds the wealth; the second generation lives like gentlemen; the third generation must start all over again."

- An old English proverb describes it this way: "There is nobbut three generations atween clogs and clogs."
- In Jewish cultures, they describe it as "rags to rags."
- In Germany, the first generation *erwerben* (creates), the second generation *vererben* (inherits) and the third generation *verberden* (destroys).

Based on conventional wisdom alone, problems seem to appear by the third generation. Research has borne this out by reporting the dismal 10%–15% succession rate to the third generation. Upon careful examination of long-lived family firms, some techniques have been successful in keeping control in the family's hands. For instance, Japan has the oldest family firms, with some of them dating back to the fifth and seventh centuries. This is made possible by their practice of officially bringing a son-in-law into the family (when needed) and having him take the family name. The business can then have a successful generational transfer without passing through blood relatives or family of origin. In the 19th century, the du Pont family maintained their wealth and control through arranged marriages between first cousins, which was common for many rich families at the time.

For the leader, succession planning means asking the hard questions, such as the following:

- Are my children the most qualified to run the business? Or is an outsider better qualified?
- Which child should I choose?
- Do my children have interest in the business?
- Would the family be better off if the business was sold?
- Which children should the company stock go to? All of them? When?
- What will I do if I retire?

In planning for succession, sentimentality should be minimized and reality faced in a businesslike manner. Numerous examples that exist detail what is at stake for the next generation and the financial viability of the firm and the family. As an example of a costly succession decision, Edgar Bronfman Jr. inherited the leadership at Seagram's (liquor) as a third-generation family member. After a costly merger into the entertainment industry with Vivendi SA, the family fortune plunged by $3 billion to $1.85 billion. The entire family has been affected by the choice of successor and his resulting decisions. The estate-planning implications of succession and tax-planning issues must be considered. Family businesses should seek professional advice from those suitably qualified in the appropriate area, such as attorneys, accountants, tax advisors, financial planners, and others.

Succession Issues

Although it may not seem readily apparent, stakeholders, including several important outside stakeholders, can have significant influences on whether the succession will be successful. In addition to the incumbent, the successor, and the family, the outside stakeholders who have influence are the customers, suppliers, bankers, and employees. If these important interests do not have faith and trust in the competency of the successor, they may pull their support, restrict their activities with the firm, or decide to withdraw their involvement altogether.

Serious dysfunctional sibling rivalries can occur if the choice of the successor were interpreted to be a result of parental favoritism or nepotism. Sibling rivalry is often an underlying cause of interpersonal conflict, one of the most serious issues a family business faces. If significant sibling rivalry is present, the business should seek help in the form of a family business consultant or from a family therapist who is experienced in business issues.

An issue that looms large for the firm's present ownership is how to equally distribute the family wealth—which is, overwhelmingly, the family business itself—to all their children. Questions arise such as whether equal ownership of the company should go to a family member who has never worked in the business and has no interest in ever working there. This can become problematic in the future for the owner-manager who may want to expand or buy equipment. The nonworking partner may disagree because of a lack of knowledge or different values, such as the desire for a larger dividend check. One survey reported 29% were planning on providing to their heirs an equal distribution of their business wealth, 22% were going to give more to those who were employed at the firm, 6% were going to give zero to nonemployees, and 25% had not decided. Only 8% planned a sale of the firm to nonfamily members.[8]

When the firm is controlled by a single, dominant family, succession problems are lessened compared with the increased complexity of when there are several branches of family involved, such as distant cousins. Unless the business is very large, it may not be able to support all the family members who want to work in the business. The early recognition of an heir is best for all parties concerned, as other family members have time to choose educational opportunities and other avenues for a career.

Leaving at the right time may be the hardest decision a founder can make, but it can be the most important decision for successful and prosperous family succession. The final legacy of the founder should be to leave on top. The new generation, with their aggressive ideas, can now take over. If a founder stays too long, the strategic decision making tends to be overly conservative, which can have a detrimental effect on the firm in terms of lost opportunities. Studies showed that the longer a current owner stayed in control, the less likely he or she would voluntarily give up control. The ideal time for an owner to retire was found to be between the ages of 50 and 60, and the ideal time for a son to step in was in the 27–33-year age range.[9] In this manner, the generational gender conflict that is often common between father and son is minimized.

The return of a retired former owner is not uncommon. Such individuals often look for a reason to return to power and authority, like a white knight coming to save the day. This situation is unfortunate for the new successor. If insiders see this situation as likely, employees and others may not fully support the successor's efforts. Some may even sabotage the decisions of the newcomer in order to bring back the previous leader and return to "the way things used to be."

Gender Issues

Research has shown that cross-gender succession, such as from a father to a daughter, is easier to accomplish than succession from father to son. The roles we each play as family members are probably the reason for this. Additional complications can arise from the ages of those involved. A considerable amount of inherent conflict is present in the relationship between father and son.

In early adulthood, the son is developing into a man and wants to prove himself, often by challenging the father. The result of this is the father can often feel threatened and resist any new ideas, even good ones, or withhold praise for positive contributions of the son. Conversely, due to the difference in roles, a father-daughter succession does not usually have those inherent conflicts. The relationship between the two is more open, the father does not feel threatened by the daughter's growing importance in the business, and the daughter does not often challenge the father as a son would. It is a much smoother transition of leadership control. (The increase in the number of women in family-owned firms is discussed in Chapter 9.)

Practices for a Successful Succession

Succession is such a vital area of importance; it is one of the key areas in which professional family business consultants have developed specializations and expertise. It may benefit a family firm to hire consultants to guide them through the process.

A key concept in succession planning is to understand that it is indeed a process, not just a one-time event. Most often, however, succession planning does not take place until the issue is forced or until it is sometimes too late, such as when a death or a serious illness forces the issue. Proper succession planning is a significant and complex process that takes years to accomplish, even when done correctly. One of the first places to begin is the identification of potential successors and the creation of development plans for them. The candidates can be assessed at a variety of stages.

The following seven succession development stages may be helpful:

1. *Positive attitude.* Attitudes toward work and the family business are formed in the first 25 years of life.
2. *Entry into the firm.* This occurs most commonly when the successor is between 20 and 30 years old and the individual fills a meaningful position in the firm.
3. *Business development.* This occurs between 25 and 35 years old, as the successor is developing and creating important relationships, skills, and abilities.

4. *Leadership development.* This phase usually occurs between 30 and 40 years of age. Skills developed during this phase are networking, team building, and shared decision making.

5. *Selection of the successor.* Among the available methods for making a choice are the incumbent chooses, the outside board makes the selection, the family executive team selects, or a consensus is formed between the family executives and the nonfamily executives.

6. *Transition of leadership.* During the transition phase, authority and responsibility are turned over to the successor. The successor takes control of the strategic direction of the firm and develops the management team.

7. *The next generation.* The development of future successors should be a constant process.[10]

Successor Development Plan

The successor, if equipped with a formal business education, may become the leader that continues the entrepreneurial nature of the firm and leads the company to increased growth through the recognition of new opportunities, new markets, expanded product lines, and even new divisions or acquisitions. It is vital, then, to choose the successor early by assessing the skills and capabilities of the successor and then to create a plan designed to develop or shore up any areas of opportunity. Many family businesses now require family members to have a university education and an MBA to fully prepare future successors for business leadership.

Large corporations have a term called "fast-tracking," where an identified leader is put through various divisions and experiences within the firm to increase learning, promote awareness, and understand how the company fits together. As an example, a fast-tracked employee would be given an overseas assignment for a short period of time, and then moved to operations, next to marketing, and so on. The purpose is to expose the future leader to as much of the organization as possible in the shortest possible amount of time. Many executives have reported their best learning experiences were when they were "thrown into the fire" and they had to learn something new. In family firms, it should be referred to as "slow-tracking." The development process of family members should be thought of more as an apprenticeship because it can often last several decades.

Creating a Succession Plan

Redefining Retirement

It can be beneficial for the senior generation to begin planning a satisfactory retirement early. Many of these leaders do not want to retire, likening it to thoughts of being put out to pasture, losing control, or even dying. It can be highly beneficial for the firm if these leaders would proactively develop outside wealth and outside interests as a way of easing the transfer of leadership to the new generation. Often, family businesses can create a significant position for the retiring leader inside the firm, where the individual can act as a public relations face of the firm. The long-established contacts they have in the industry and the community are valuable assets in this position. Another option could put the founder who steps down in charge of the philanthropic arm of the family business. One Southern California printing company, now run by a five-member, second-generation sibling partnership, uses their founder mother as the public relations face of the firm at chamber of commerce events and as a de facto salesperson in the local community.

A resourceful and constructive use for the former leader is to use their acquired talents to develop new products or new divisions at the family business. Although a nonfamily business example, when Bill Gates stepped back from day-to-day operations at Microsoft, he took on the title of chief visionary. Freed from the grind of his daily responsibilities, he then had time to focus on areas of strategic importance for Microsoft. When he left that position, he focused full time on the Bill and Melinda Gates Foundation. Although most family businesses do not have that level of charitable giving available, a smaller foundation at a more localized level could be a tremendous asset for the firm.

The danger of a poorly planned retirement is that the senior leader does not fully retire and continues to meddle in the business. This murky role confuses stakeholders, employees, customers, and suppliers regarding who is in charge, and it undermines the current leadership, which must solidify its power and authority. This is a common reason successors become frustrated and may even leave the firm, thus placing the company's continued future in serious doubt. If the retiring leader has a positive role to be proud of, making a valuable contribution to the continuing organization, the retiring executive is more likely to enjoy the new role and improve the chances for a successful succession.

Building wealth outside the family business is helpful to aid in succession and as an insurance policy in case of disruption of the business. Over 90% of family businesses have their entire wealth invested in the company: In other words, all their eggs are in one basket. If the business goes down, the all the family's wealth dissolves. By having outside investments and using business diversification, the family business eases the way for succession. The original leaders do not necessarily require significant payments from the succeeding generation to maintain their lifestyle, which could burden the new leadership with significant debt. One common practice associated with stepping down is for the previous generation to purchase the real estate associated with the business and then lease it back to the business, thereby providing a stable retirement income.

Estate Planning

It is not the purpose of this book to make recommendations for estate and tax planning purposes. Professionals (tax attorneys, accountants, estate planners) should be consulted. The guidelines change often. This subject matter is so vitally important, the success or failure of the business rides on successful estate planning for future generations to succeed.

The majority of family firms rely on insurance to pay the tax liability upon generational transfer. Approximately 50% of survey respondents regularly utilize the gift exclusion as an estate planning tool to gift company stock to heirs. Approximately two-thirds of other generations know the estate plan intentions in regard to company shares.[11]

As of December 22, 2017, the Tax Cut and Jobs Act was signed into law. The analysts are working hard to see what this means for family business owners and their families. Presently, it looks as if starting in 2018, the basic exclusion for gifts, estate, and generation skipping tax transfers has been doubled from $5 million to $10 million. After 2026, it goes back to $5 million. The annual exclusion for gifts appears to be $15,000 starting in 2018 and then adjusted for inflation.[12]

Many firms are forced to sell all or parts of their organization in order to satisfy estate tax requirements. For example, the Los Angeles Dodgers were forced to sell when the O'Malley family was faced with severe estate tax issues. An expense not commonly known to family-owned businesses is the total cost, and thus the cash needed, to successfully navigate a succession transition following the death of the former generation. Expenses often overlooked include CPA and attorney fees, insurance, taxes, and costs for professional advisors. The need for a business valuation is both critical and inevitable.

Family business owners often want to divide the ownership equally among all the children. However, equal ownership is especially problematic when inactive shareholders have an equal vote. If an outside shareholder's concern is for short-term dividend maximization, the individual may tend to vote down capital outlays for expansion, diversification, or equipment, causing problems for the owner-manager in effectively growing and operating the business.

By the third generation, imbalance in ownership may occur, with a larger family having divided ownership, which gives them a smaller share of ownership per family member. Conversely, a smaller family or an unmarried or childless individual would have a significantly larger percentage of ownership and control. As shown by the Shareholder Complexity Diagram (see Figure 6.1), the founder passes the shares on to each of the three offspring equally. By the third generation, due to varying family sizes, cousin 3 has a significantly larger percentage of ownership than do cousins 1, 2, 4, 5, and 6. Potential conflicts exist with this type of ownership distribution. Imagine if the family firm is successful enough to make it to the fourth generation of ownership: certain branches of the

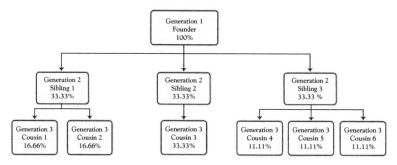

Figure 6.1. Shareholder complexity diagram.

family would be significantly more powerful than others, simply due to the concentration of ownership.

Solutions

Nonvoting Stock

One of the techniques estate planners suggest in succession planning with family firms is the creation of nonvoting stock. Inactive family members can be owners of the firm, but not decision makers in the firm. The technique has negative aspects associated with it as well, especially when a new generation of descendants of inactive family members becomes active in the family firm. Here, again, the family business should consult a specialized attorney.

Pruning the Family Tree

Studying the history of long-term successful family firms often provides visible evidence of family members or branches of the family being bought out. This technique can enable a family firm to avoid ownership dispersion by maintaining control of the business in one branch of the family. It allows inactive shareholders to turn their investments into cash and can help avoid the problem of having a plethora of owners a few generations in the future. Situations to avoid might include examples such as the sixth-generation family firm McIlhenny Co. (Tabasco sauce). The company has 145 shareholders—mostly family. The English family firm that owns Clarks Shoes at one time had over 1,000 family shareholders. The divergent motives of family members became problematic and the family narrowly averted an outright sale.[13] Pruning one of the third-generation family branches shown in the shareholder complexity diagram in Figure 6.1 may be a satisfactory solution to the problem of ownership imbalance.

The pruning strategy is not without risk, however. Such actions can have the opposite effect by causing significant family conflict to the point of family members not speaking to each other. Most often, the concerns revolve around disagreements concerning the fair market value of shares.

Due to the limited liquidity of the shares and the prohibition of selling stock to nonfamily members, this can be a recipe for disagreement.[14]

Trusts

Family firms in the United States often have the company shares held in family trusts. The purpose is to help manage the transition from one generation to the next. Estate planning, especially the financial and tax planning aspects of succession, is extremely complex. Adding to the complexity is the fact that each year changes in the tax code amend what is allowed or disallowed, new techniques are created, new rulings are made by the taxation bodies, and other techniques fall out of favor. The bottom line for family members is to have professional help in these matters. If a trust is found to be invalid, the entire estate may need to go through probate, which is extremely expensive and very time-consuming. The firm's certified public accountant and tax attorney should be consulted and made aware of the family's preferences in regards to succession. The estate plan should be reviewed annually and updated as necessary to ensure it is still valid and that legislative changes have not placed the plan's success at risk.

Employee Stock Ownership Plans

Many family firms have successfully utilized employee stock ownership plans (ESOPs). This tool is especially useful when a family owner does not have heirs or, most importantly, the owner wants to take care of long-term valued employees. The employees can buy in over a period of time and eventually end up controlling the firm. The owner is able to turn an illiquid asset into cash. This is an especially difficult method and must be discussed with an experienced professional.

Exit Strategies

Depending on the purpose of the family business, such as whether the intent is to pass the business on to future generations or to build financial wealth, strategic thought should be devoted to the exit strategy. The most apparent strategy is to have a succession from one generation of the family to the next. If no successor can be identified, or no family member is interested, the family may need to consider a sale to a nonfamily employee or to an outsider. This might be the time that the family firm institutes nonfamily management and steps away from day-to-day management responsibilities.

Although it is easier said than done, the most opportune time to sell the firm and thus to obtain the highest value is when the business is doing well. Many families wait until the wolf is at the door before considering a sale. By this time, it may be too late, and the destruction of wealth can be devastating to the family. This is obviously an emotion-filled topic for many families, but it should be explored at family meetings. The need to understand the goals of the succeeding generations in regard to selling the business is critical. Should a sale be considered? When? Under what circumstances? What would the process be?

One large California construction firm had a fully completed succession from the original sibling partnership to the second generation at a significantly reduced price compared with the firm's outside value. Within just a few years, the successors sold the firm to a larger company and pocketed the windfall. Needless to say, the first generation was not pleased. It would be beneficial to assess everyone's views and long-term goals regarding a sale of the firm.

Selling the Business

There are certain instances where the sale of the business to nonfamily members is justified: after an exhaustive search when no qualified family candidates are located or no candidates are available for development. The second scenario occurs when the business environment has changed so extensively that the firm is unable to compete or family members are unwilling or unable to invest in new technology to allow the business to compete. Family members should consider a sale of the firm rather than allowing the business to limp along toward a slow death. The family investment and wealth can be saved rather than lost due to the family's inability to face the inevitability of business failure.

If the family has decided to sell the firm, it can often become an extended process in order to obtain the highest value. The financial reports should show increasing sales and they need to be accurate for a minimum of 3 years (ideally, 5 years). This can be problematic, as many private firms' lavish perks on family members, such as expensive company cars, technology products (e.g., computers and cell phones), travel, restaurants, entertainment, clothing, and personal and professional services. Justification for these purchases is often tax minimization (as these items can be written off as a business expense rather than be given to the owners in the form of salary or income). The vast majority of private firms practice highly aggressive tax minimization strategies. The financial reports then show the business to look less profitable than it actually is, which has the effect of lowering the firm's value to potential outside purchasers. Extensive time, up to several years, may be required to make the needed changes from a tax minimization strategy to a sale maximization strategy.

The valuation of the firm is a technical undertaking. The firm's accountant will be involved, as will its attorneys and, more than likely, an outside business brokerage firm, who will represent and promote the firm to possible interested parties.

The Role of the Spouse

Since the majority of family-owned businesses are male dominated, this section discussed the important role that a wife or female partner has in the business. However, family firms owned by women are increasing; the spouse may now increasingly be a male. The spouse has usually taken on the role of chief caregiver to the family's needs at home, allowing the marital partner to concentrate on running the business. Because of this role, the female spouse has been given the term CEO (chief emotional officer). The spouse plays a necessary and vital role in the healthy functioning of the family. If the children are fighting with each other or angry with their father, the mother often listens to the issues and, if needed, mediates. Spouses may broker discussions or use their influence on their spouse to provide awareness of situations within the family that may have an adverse impact on the business and thus the extended family. It is for this reason the spouses should be welcomed at the family council and at all other family meetings.

CHAPTER 7

Governance, Advisors, and Boards

To understand the complexities of family business, it is important to understand its governance and systems. There are three basic forms of family business governance: the controlling owner, the sibling partnership, and the cousin consortium. The latter is usually characterized by members of at least three generations.[1] As the business matures and progresses through the stages of the business life cycle, more family stakeholders become involved. With the three subsystems in mind (owners, managers, and family members), it is easy to understand the differences between family members who are in different subsystems. For instance, a family member who is an owner but not an employee may be more inclined to consider an offer from an outsider to purchase the business than a family member who is both an owner and a member of the management who depends on the business for livelihood. The controlling owner may not be willing to pay high salaries to employees who are family members but who are not also owners.

The purpose of a *family-first* business is to benefit the family only. Employment is often considered a birthright and nepotism is common. Valuable perquisites of employment are the norm and pay is not usually based on merit. The family is the priority, not the business. A *management-first* business is associated with professional supervision of the firm. In this structure, it is common to see nonfamily management in charge. Family members need to undergo interviews and must be qualified in order to join the family firm. *Ownership-first* businesses place emphasis on the shareholders. These shareholders are often nonemployed family members or members of the larger cousin coalition, and they have a short-term financial outlook.[2] Poza emphasized that the ideal scenario is to have a balance among each of the three systems.

Governance Vehicles

There are numerous governance vehicles for the family to utilize. They are designed for the family to have a way of providing discussion and communication with each other and as a way to pass their agreed priorities and wishes to the firm management. Table 9.1 presents informal governance vehicles designed to increase family communication.

Family Meetings

Of all the tools or techniques a family business has at its disposal, instituting family meetings may be the easiest, and it can have the greatest positive impact on the future of the firm and the family. Most family businesses do not have good communication among the family members. The first generation commonly likes to make business decisions alone, and they often do not discuss how they arrived at their decisions. This may irritate other family members, some of whom may have different viewpoints on the issue. By having family meetings, families can discuss issues, problems, and opportunities and use the time to catch up with members who may now be adult family members leading separate lives, with families of their own. Family members who are owners but are not employed at the family business often feel out of the loop on many issues and decisions. The family meeting is a way to foster family togetherness and increase communication among members of the family.

To get the greatest benefit from the family meeting, a facilitator should be present to ensure the meeting runs smoothly. The facilitator should not stifle creativity or be confrontational, and he or she should encourage everyone to discuss and share issues, ideas, or concerns. It is good to use an agenda and have a note taker provide a written record of any decisions or agreements. The meetings should be scheduled regularly, possibly every quarter or every 2 months, and all family members should be invited.

Many entrepreneurial family firms, such as relatively new start-ups, can benefit from this simple meeting. At the entrepreneurial stage in a family firm, the founders are usually working long hours, changes are ever present, and the environment is fast paced. Business ideas and issues are decided and then changed. The family meeting is a forum designed to increase communication among all family members, which can prevent confusion, dissension, or conflict. The most important concept is that the meeting is a vehicle for increased communication. As long as there are healthy dialogue and open avenues of communication, it is difficult to have conflict and serious dysfunction. When family members do not talk, serious dysfunction is more likely to occur.

Family Constitution

The family constitution is a document that lists the mission and vision of the firm and spells out the family commitment to continuity, responsibilities of ownership, conflict resolution procedures, as well as the company policies and procedures on such important issues as family employment, including hiring, retirement, and terminations. The constitution includes buy-sell agreements, shareholder policies, role of spouses and nonfamily members in the firm, and handling of unemployed family business members. Procedures for when a family member develops a drug or alcohol problem or becomes disabled, rules of ownership such as procedures for selling shares, noncompete agreements, job descriptions for top management positions, and rules of governance are among the many other issues addressed. The critical function of the constitution is to document family discussion and input and to have discussed the issues *before* being forced to decide when the family has a crisis and emotions are running high. Interestingly, the vast majority of family businesses do not have this all-important document. In addition to the aforementioned items, the following other considerations should be discussed for inclusion in a family constitution:

- A share liquidity policy, including buybacks and dividends
- A family remuneration policy
- A procedure for making decisions (e.g., consensus, vote) and who will make them
- Officer's roles and responsibilities
- Employee roles and responsibilities
- A family member termination policy
- The number of times boards, councils, and the family will meet
- Establishment of an annual family retreat
- Educational reimbursement policy for family members

- A policy for settling disputes or conflict among family members specifying who will settle the dispute, such as the outside board of advisors or family council
- A family member exit policy
- Possible exit strategies for the business
- Establishment of a board of advisors or directors and their role
- Number and role of family members on the boards
- Establishment of a family council and its responsibilities and roles
- Reporting structure for family members
- Evaluation structure and procedures for family members, indicating who will perform the evaluations
- Human resources policies for all hires, family and nonfamily

The list is full of emotionally charged issues and items for discussion. It will take several meetings of the family and days to weeks of discussions to arrive at a document the family can agree on. Many families agree it is time well spent and that is vital to discuss before serious issues arise.

Family Councils

Instituting a family council is a significantly positive step toward managing the business in a more rational and professional manner. The family council is more formal than the family meeting. The purpose of the council is to present the *family* issues of running the business. The family council is where problems, concerns, issues, and opportunities are presented and discussed, alternatives are weighed, and decisions are made. In a family council, the family usually takes a vote, and decisions are made either by a simple majority or by consensus. Some families strive for unanimity, which can tend to delay decisions but has been found to increase family unity. For the family council to be effective, all members must recognize the council is the proper time and place to present their point of view. One of the major positive attributes of the family council is that family members agree to abide by the decision of the council (even if they disagree with it or are on the losing end of the vote) and consent to not grumble about it outside of the meeting but instead show support and unity for the family decision. The decisions of the family council are then presented to the board of directors in larger family firms for their enactment.

The creation of a family council can be difficult to manage initially. Research on family council effectiveness shows that for the council to work well, it often needs to be facilitated by a professional. This enables the meetings to be more productive and it holds members accountable for following through on decisions.[3] It can be a tremendous adjustment for the owner-manager who manages in a paternalistic manner to relinquish decision-making power and authority to the council. Moving to a more professional and rational method of decision making has been shown to increase family business longevity. By the third generation, the larger number of family members, with multiple cousins and some second-generation members still active, presents the need for a formal democratic voting process.

Generational Meetings

Specific generational meetings are useful to increase communication with cohorts. It is easy to see how a member of the second generation may have the same issues as other second-generation members. Family business consultants and university-based family business centers have found that when providing a workshop, dividing the participants into specific cohort groups accomplishes two important functions. First, participants feel free to discuss their issues in a safe environment, free from criticism by a family member of a different generation. Second, the other members in the cohort group can usually relate to the issue, since they are more than likely experiencing a similar issue. The group members realize they are not alone and others may feel the same way.

Consultants often use this approach to start a family retreat and then bring the family back together to discuss the issues. It is enlightening and somewhat humorous to hear the first-generation cohort members express desire for the second generation to become more aggressive and take more responsibility and then to hear the second-generation members trading stories of the resulting pain of when they did attempt to take more responsibility!

Once a month, on a Sunday evening, all the third-generation Cathy family members (cousin consortium) of the Chick-fil-A restaurant chain have a telephone conference call. The purpose of the call is to share updates, stay in contact, and build relationships with cousins based all over the country. The activity fosters a sense of third-generation community and closeness and increases the ability to relate one to another. When these distant cousins rise to power within the corporation, they will have relationships based on criteria other than just the family business.

Professional Advisors

Advisors can be divided by advisors inside the firm and outside the firm. Inside advisors consist of relatives and key nonfamily employees who work in the family business. The firm's outside advisors consist of professionals such as the accountant, the lawyer, and family business consultants who specialize in helping family businesses navigate through issues that are unique to family firms. When the first family business consultancies formed, they were often former members of other family businesses who had experience dealing with particular issues. The accountants became involved with consulting, since a large part of their practice was family

Table 7.1. Family Business Corporate Governance Vehicles

	Family meeting	Family council	Generational meeting
Stage	Founders	Sibling partnership Cousin consortium	Sibling partnership Cousin consortium
Status	Informal	More formal	Informal
Membership	Usually entails key family management. Often open to all family members in larger firms.	Family members are sometimes elected by the family (in large firms). Other membership criteria can be set by the family. Often it is open to all.	Open to members of each specific generation.
Size	Small	Depends on membership criteria. Ideally 5–9 members.	Depends on family size.
Number of annual meetings	Due to its fast growth and need to take advantage of opportunities, family meetings may be called often, up to several times a week.	1–2 times per year	As often as needed, usually 2–6 times per year

businesses and their clients were asking for help and advice. The lawyers became involved in tax planning, estate planning, and succession as well.

By far, the most utilized and highly ranked professional advisor to family businesses is the accountant. This may be due to a lack of financial skills, especially among the first generation. Most family businesses have a good relationship with their CPA and utilize their accountant for valued financial advice. The company attorney is usually consulted only when a legal need arises or when discussing succession. The banker is third most often used, and outside business peers are also consulted.

Consultants

Family business consultancies today are usually multiconsultant teams in firms that can provide full services to a prospective client. The consultancies usually have a counselor or therapist to deal with interpersonal conflict issues that threaten to divide the business, a CPA for financial issues, a lawyer, and general organizational development or organizational behavior professionals who can help guide a firm through management issues such as succession or instituting a board of advisors. Succession planning is the most common reason for a firm to contact a consultant. The next is conflict management, followed by teamwork issues.

Upon entering a consultancy arrangement with a family firm, one of the first things a family business consultant does is have the family take one of the personality instruments, such as the Myers-Briggs Personality Type Index (MBTI). These are excellent tools to help understand the differences between the various family members. Results detail how people prefer to make their decisions, how they gather their information, how they gain their energy (extroversion or introversion), and how they like to interact with the external environment. Personality instruments are excellent tools for aiding in conflict management and promoting team building. Usually one day of a certified facilitator leading the family through the various personality types and explaining the differences can lead to a significant amount of relationship improvement and improvement in working effectiveness.

Boards of Advisors

These voluntary and informal boards are made up of respected business owners; trusted professionals, such as bankers, certified public accountants (CPAs), and attorneys; and respected friends and business associates. The board acts as a sounding board and gives advice to the business. The business is under no obligation to accept the recommendations; the board has no formal authority due to lack of ownership. Most family firms do not utilize this helpful tool; however, some family firms, especially in the second generation, use a de facto board of advisors when they consult with other respected professionals in the community and in their social network. Some family business CEOs have benefitted from attending a CEO forum in their local area and gaining advice and input from it.

Boards of Directors

In the United States, every corporation is required to have a board of directors. In family firms, the board roles are usually filled by the owners. They are mandated to list certain officers on the incorporation papers and to meet at least once a year. In a nonfamily firm, the board of directors has significant responsibility and formal authority to make recommendations and decisions, as well as to have them instituted. They have hiring and termination authority over the CEO. They are paid positions and usually contain outside members. The purpose of the board is to provide a system of checks and balances and to help ensure accountability.

Due to the ethical lapses exhibited by the collapse of Tyco, Enron, Arthur Andersen, and WorldCom, among many others, the Sarbanes-Oxley Financial Accountability Act was instituted. One of the outcomes of the legislation was strengthened guidelines for boards of directors. A board of directors must have outside independent directors in order to provide the best guidance and oversight. If the board is dominated by insiders, the thinking can become insulated and narrow and may turn a blind eye to unethical or questionable behavior. The Sarbanes-Oxley legislation delineates the board's responsibilities and now holds board members accountable for behaving responsibly and providing good oversight of the corporation, particularly in financial matters. There is now significant legal and financial liability associated with being a board member, as they can now be held accountable for any firm mismanagement.

Most family firms do not properly use boards of directors; however, family businesses with strong boards of directors have improved decision-making ability. The research is clear on this point. This is partially due to the beneficial aspects of conflict. Diversity of opinion and good debate lead to members having their say and arguing a valid point. Points of view are put forth that normally could have been stifled. By hearing a variety of ideas and solutions to problems, family businesses make better decisions.

To foster good debate, the board must have nonfamily members serving on it, as well as people from outside the firm. The usefulness of a board of directors whose membership consists of those with significant experience outside the family or outside the business is especially apparent when the firm is run by a charismatic and powerfully assertive founder or other family member. A broader range of ideas, suggestions, and recommendations can now be discussed, especially those not seen as favorable by the family member in control. Reflect how difficult it would be to vote against your father or other relative, especially if this relative were your boss, and when your income, wealth, and future employment is intertwined.

The vast majority of firms who have a board of directors rate its contribution as good to excellent. Most of the boards meet only once or twice a year, and just 29% of boards of directors meet three or more times a year.[4] Instituting a board of directors is a significant area of opportunity for many family firms to improve their management and company performance. A major responsibility of the board is to look at the business *separately* from the needs of the family. The needs of the family are discussed in the family council. The council makes recommendations to the board of directors on behalf of the family.

Most Trusted Advisor

In the past, the most trusted family business advisor has been the financial accountant. Recently, the most trusted advisor has been shown to be the spouse. The spouse also plays a significant role as *chief emotional officer* of the family. This role has traditionally been filled by the wife or mother of the CEO. Research has shown the importance of this role, as the success of the family business often depends on support from spouses. Often, spouses will mediate interpersonal conflict between family members and, in essence, act as the glue to hold the family tightly together. You may remember *consigliore*, or *counselor*, was the title of Robert Duvall's character in *The Godfather*. The most trusted advisor acts as a counselor to the family business owner.

CHAPTER 8

Success Tips for Family Business Owners, Employers, and Professionals

Danny Miller and Isabelle Le Breton-Miller studied 46 successful family businesses, including Wal-Mart, Nordstrom's, Bechtel, Coors, Corning, Fidelity Investments, Tyson, IKEA, and Cargill. The researchers' purpose was to uncover what made these firms so successful and gave them the ability to thrive as family firms. They arrived at what they called the four Cs: *continuity* (a long-term focus), *community* (a strong cohesive team focused on values), *connection* (a deep relationship with key stakeholders such as the local community and suppliers), and *command* (an empowered top management team unfettered by bureaucratic rules, thus enabling them to move fast and seize opportunities).[1]

To survive for multiple generations, a family business needs enough flexibility to accept transition and the ability to recognize opportunity when the markets or business environment has changed.

Family Employment Policies

Although no hard research data exists yet, consultants who advise family-owned businesses increasingly suggest that the next generation of family leaders should not enter the family firm until first working outside the company. Many professionally managed family firms subscribe to this excellent practice. When the child wishes to enter the business, employees and parents alike will have an increased level of respect for him or her. Ideally, the sons or daughters should work in a business where they will develop new knowledge or skills or in a firm in a different market that can help them when they enter the family firm. For example, it would be beneficial for younger family members to have worked in a retail grocery chain before entering the family's grocery distribution business. Many firms require the family member to receive at least one promotion at the firm in order to demonstrate the individual is qualified and will be able to make a valued contribution to the firm. Then the family member is seen as adding significant value and is accepted as a deserving member of the team.

Many family firms have instituted policies and procedures to govern the hiring of family members and to indicate what is required before family members enter the family business. Many businesses require children of business owners to obtain a university education and work outside the family firm for a period of 2–3 years before entering the family business. There are multiple reasons why consultants recommend the outside work experience, but most revolve around respect, competence, and confidence among the following three stakeholders:

- *Employees.* When the children of the owner first arrive at the company, the existing employees believe it is mainly due to their last name. If the job is not earned or deserved, the existing employees will not respect the family prodigy, and disruptive conflict can flare up. By arriving at the company fully qualified, employees will more readily accept the offspring rather than derail them or engage in nonproductive interpersonal conflict.
- *Parents.* Very often, parents have a difficult time accepting their son or daughter in the family business at anything other than employee status. This is due to the established family roles. (Let's face it, they have changed their diapers.) It can be a difficult transition for the parents to see their children as valuable members of the business who can make a contribution, rather than as the dumb kid who threw a rock through the church window (like the author did). This transition can be significantly eased by the children finding success outside the family business and entering the business with increased knowledge, skills, and management techniques that can add value and help the business grow or become more efficient.
- *Themselves.* The young family business leader will have more confidence upon entering the family business if he or she has

succeeded elsewhere. Such second-generation members will know it is due to themselves as individuals and not their name or family connections. Even if the next-generation member has outside business experience, some current stakeholders will still harbor suspicions or a bias that the job may not be deserved. The extra self-confidence gained by working outside the firm is priceless.

The family employment policies are documented in the family constitution, and this document should also spell out policies for family employee appraisals, feedback, mentoring, and procedures for developing career plans. Some firms have family members report to nonfamily managers to avoid possible conflict of interest or nepotism issues.

Start the Children Early in the Family Business

Many entrepreneurs got their start by working in the family business when they were young. Statistics show that some stay in the family business, some pursue their own career ambitions, and others move on to start their own entrepreneurial ventures. However, the child of a business owner is two to three times more likely to become self-employed than the child of a nonbusiness owner. In fact, those youths who were actively involved in the family business tend to do better. Business owners who had previously worked in the family business were associated with a lower probability of business closure, a 40% increase in sales, and a higher probability of profits.[2]

Several of today's business moguls are good examples of entrepreneurs who learned the meaning of hard work early in life. Warren Buffett, one of the richest people in the United States, had a paper route at age 13; his father was a self-employed insurance and investment broker. *Forbes* 400 member Donald Trump learned the real estate business from his father; his children are now learning it from him. CNN founder Ted Turner learned the media business working in his dad's billboard company.

Nonfamily Employees

Most family firms cannot exist by solely employing family members. Nonfamily employees are a time proven, dependable, and important part of the labor pool. Employees feel they are treated better at family firms than at nonfamily firms. In addition, the use of performance based pay, extensive selection processes, in-house training and development, employee empowerment, and job enrichment initiatives have been shown by family firms who use these practices to outperform nonfamily firms. Conversely, family firms not using employee positive behaviors do not outperform their nonfamily peers.[3] The contribution of nonfamily employees can be a competitive advantage for family firms.

- All is not good news in the employment area, however. In a study of 278 small family owned business in Pennsylvania, 53% of the respondents did not have professional human resources practices in place.
- Slightly less than 25% had written job descriptions outlining responsibilities, minimum qualifications and reporting structure for each position in the business. Only 16 percent conduct formal performance reviews, and 19 percent have a bonus structure in effect.[4]

According to a 2015 survey, 60% of family business respondents cited recruitment of skilled personnel as their most significant challenge.[5]

Unfortunately, another survey shows nonfamily employees are less confident in the next generation of family leadership.[6] With the important contribution of nonfamily employees to the positive performance of the family firm, professional human resource practices should be followed. This seems to be an area of opportunity for family business's to overcome by being more professional.

Tips for Success

For a family business to succeed and advance to the next level, the following tasks have been shown to increase professionalism and business success. By instituting even *some* of these, a family business will go a long way toward increasing its effectiveness and chances for long-term success.

- Create the family mission statement. Why does the business exist? What is its purpose?
- Create processes to facilitate discussions (e.g., family meetings, family retreats, council, shareholders meetings, etc.).
- Create a strategic plan.
- Institute influential boards.
- Create policies and procedures that detail family members' roles (i.e., family constitution).
- Hire nonfamily professional managers.
- Institute the succession planning process.
- Create a fair and appropriate equity arrangement that takes into consideration those family members active in the management of the business.

In a survey, family business leaders were asked the following question: "Which of the following characteristics do you think are most important for success in a family business?" Clear succession planning, shared objectives, and conflict resolution score high, pointing to the need for and importance of good, open communication:[7]

- Clear succession plans: 47%
- Clear and shared objectives: 44%
- Strong leadership: 41%
- Ability to resolve conflicts quickly and effectively: 30%
- Ownership restricted to family members: 26%
- Ability to take risks: 20%
- Strong governance structure: 19%
- Willingness to recruit outsiders: 15%

Appendix D lists a series of important discussion questions that should be asked of family firms and their members. These questions can help with the creation of the family constitution and can be used at family council meetings or family retreats.

What Family Business Professionals Need to Know

There are cautions for the various professionals who view family businesses as potential customers, such as family business advisors, attorneys, accountants, financial services firms, insurance firms, and small business suppliers. Suppliers can often become frustrated working with family businesses. They question why the family takes so long to make a decision, why so many people are involved, and why their decisions sometimes do not make logical business sense.

When the firm is operated by the first generation, usually a single founder with sole discretion authority, the decisions can happen quickly, with little apparent difference between this type of business and any other business of its size. In second- and third-generation firms, professionals can expect a longer decision period because multiple family members are involved. The professional should plan for delays based on the differences in goals and objectives among family members. Professionals should take notice of the number of involved family members at the firm. The decision process is slowed significantly when three or more family members are involved in the decision. Depending on the product or service offered, the decision times are usually lengthened if the family perceives the decision as expensive (or risky) when it concerns other family members or if the price of failure is high.

A tool was created to help family business professionals and suppliers understand where each family business lies in regard to decision making for various products and services (see Figure 8.1). This tool shows how each decision area increases in complexity in a fairly linear fashion, from small, everyday (programmed) decisions with one or two involved family members, to small programmed decisions with three or more involved family members, up to the larger nonprogrammed (less common, not previously made) decisions with one or two involved family members. Once the nonprogrammed decision area reaches family member involvement of three or more people, the complexity grows exponentially in an extreme nonlinear fashion.

When a professional calls on a specific family business, he or she should first understand how the products or services offered will be perceived by the business.

1. Is it a quick and relatively easy type of everyday purchase such as janitorial services or stationery, which will not involve other family members?

2. Conversely, could the family perceive it as risky, costly, or requiring a large capital outlay?

3. Would other family members want to be involved in the decision based on the previously mentioned factors?

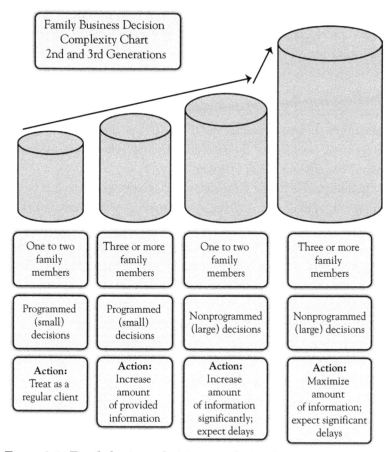

Figure 8.1. Family business decision complexity chart.

The chart is a tool allowing family business professionals to assess the level of their customer's firm and the corresponding action necessary to provide the firm with the required information to enable a decision.

Source: Alderson (2009).

4. Would it affect a larger number of family members than just the individual who sees the presentation?

5. Could the decision affect the family reputation in the community?

After the products and services have been analyzed, the particular family business should be assessed as to where the business decision should be located on the chart. As the level of complexity increases, the professional should be prepared for a longer decision time, the involvement of more family members, and a need for more information. If the professional cannot make a presentation to all family members, then he or she must depend on the family business contact to disseminate the information to all concerned members. The professional may facilitate this process by asking what information would be helpful to other family members, by providing multiple copies of brochures or documents, and by presenting a much more in-depth informative report, addressing as many of the family's potential questions and concerns as possible. In this manner, every family member can be provided with the information to answer individual questions and or concerns.

In the broad search for information and knowledge undertaken by the firm as part of its decision making, the professional would be well advised to provide an abundance of information, bordering on the minutia. Such abundant information may provide the family the sense of comfort they need to collect as much information and knowledge as possible. Previous customer recommendations, testimonials, guarantees, warrantees, known business associates, and conversations with or special attention from key company executives can all help to enable the family business to reach a knowledge comfort level. By understanding the history, makeup, and structure of the family business and its key decision makers, professionals can adjust their proposals and provide more information in order to increase the family's knowledge and comfort level, thereby helping involved family members make a knowledgeable decision. Additionally, the professional can become a more valuable resource for his or her customers. Such value may increase business within the family business area, gaining a competitive advantage over those competitors without knowledge of family business decision making.

One sibling partnership (composed of five owners) I consulted with in Southern California was carefully reviewing the specifications for a multimillion-dollar piece of machinery after previously buying similar machinery that did not perform as promised and experiencing years of an expensive legal battle. Is anyone surprised that the firm's owners requested a personal conversation and guarantee with the president of the machinery manufacturer? This was the final piece of information the family needed in order to feel comfortable with their purchasing decision. The machinery firm thought it an odd request. However, it is not odd when the background information is reviewed:

- There are 5 second-generation family decision makers.
- All worked in the business.
- The founder is still involved.
- The previous machinery purchase almost crippled them financially.

Businesses that target family firms and have a thorough understanding of their potential client's needs, wants, and lengthened decision process may develop a significant competitive advantage. (Yes, the president's meeting sealed the deal, and the family made the purchase.)

CHAPTER 9

Trends in Family Business and Future Research

The Increasing Presence of Women in Family Business

One of the most important changes within family business has been the significant increase of women in management and ownership. In the past, in most societies, it was the norm for the business to be passed on to the oldest son (primogeniture) upon the retirement or death of the founder. Up until 20 years ago, women were not usually considered to head the family business, especially in countries that had male-dominated cultures. Only if there were no male successors were the women considered. Another barrier to women is if the family business is in an industry that is thought of as more masculine oriented (e.g., automotive parts manufacturing or construction) compared to a more feminine industry (e.g., fashion or services).

In a 2007 survey by MassMutual Financial Group, 24% of surveyed family firms in 2007 had a woman CEO, up from only 10% in 2002. Thirty-four percent of CEOs surveyed said the company's next CEO might be a woman. According to the study, these are substantial businesses, having $26.9 million in average annual revenues, with some reporting $1 billion in sales. Moreover, the report stated that women-owned businesses were more likely to focus on succession planning, to have a 40% lower rate of family-member attrition, to be more fiscally conservative, and to carry less debt than male-owned businesses. In 1994, according to another survey, 2% of CEOs in family businesses were women. In 2005, 9.5% of family business heads were women.[1]

In a 2015 study by the consulting firm Ernst & Young consisting of 525 of the World's largest and oldest family owned firms, 70% of respondents noted they were considering a woman for their next CEO, and 30% said they were strongly considering a woman for the top job.

Moreover, 55% reported at least one woman on the board, and 16% of board member are women. In a positive development 22% of surveyed firms stated 22% of their top management is women, compared with only 12.9% average of all firms in general.[2]

Daughters are now considered to be one the most underutilized resources in family businesses. To encourage the next generation of women to be valuable members of the business, potential female successors should be nurtured by assimilation into the family firm, mentoring, sharing in important tacit knowledge, and having positive role models within the business.

Women considering entrance into their own or their family's business have a large opportunity. The rate of women CEOs is significantly higher in family firms than nonfamily firms. Experienced and talented women who become tired of bumping up against the proverbial glass ceiling, may consider the family business. The EY survey (2015) reported that 41% of respondents said female family members have become more interested in the family business. This is a very positive development for the success of family firms.

The controlling owner of 150 plus year old Heineken NV is an example of successful woman ownership. Charlene de Carvalho-Heineken was a stay at home mother of five who had no interest in working at what would become the worlds third largest brewer. Sitting on the board since 1988, she inherited a 51% controlling interest in the firm when her father died in in 2012. She, along with her husband have replaced the CEO, and gone on an acquisition drive of other brands (Dos Equis, Bohemia, and Lagunitas). She also had the courage of conviction to turn down a buyout offer from the worlds second largest brewer SABMiller. Her goal is the same as her fathers; to allow the company to prosper and keep it independent so she can pass it on to her children. She is the wealthiest person in the Netherlands.

Gina Rinehart is Australia's richest woman. She took her fathers bankrupt estate and built it into a large iron ore producer. She is seen as tough and often controversial, and was sued by two of her four children regarding their trust. Her business acumen is not in doubt. She now owns part of a TV station and has expanded from mining into cattle.

The reclusive Grandaughter of the In-N-Out chain of fast food restaurants in the Western United States is considered to be the youngest billionaire in the country. She inherited 50% of the privately held company when she turned 30. When she turned 35, she inherited most of the rest of the stock. The company is valued at $1.3 billion. The firm was started by her grandparents in 1948. She has vowed to keep the company private and not franchise in keeping with her grandparents values. She is very private due to two attempted abduction attempts.[3]

Another excellent example of women ownership comes from a Columbian manufacturing company whose patriarch chose the second born son to take over upon the founders retirement (the right of primogeniture is very common in Latin American countries). The son was chosen over the daughter who was an engineer, an MBA, and who grew up walking around the shop floor with her father since she was five years old. The son was a playboy with a taste for illicit substances, and not much interest in the business. When business declined, the father replaced the son with the very qualified daughter, and the company has been very successful as a result.

University Education

Stetson University in Florida was the first university to offer both a major and a minor in family business management. Now students are able to study family business at over 100 universities throughout the United States and around the world. There are approximately 100 university-based family business centers in the United States and over 150 throughout the world. The first centers were founded at Oregon State University and Kennesaw State University in Georgia. This was based on demand from many struggling family business owners who needed specific advice about how to manage *their* business, not the types of businesses that are routinely profiled in *Businessweek*, in *Fortune* magazine, or on the financial news channels. The family business centers (FBCs) have various kinds of resources, such as workshops, seminars, consulting, and conflict management tools, to help family firms navigate through the complex issues they face.

The Need for Financial Management

Many of the first-generation entrepreneurial founders did not have a formal university education. However, it is interesting that they strongly encourage their children to gain an education. A significant percentage of students at private universities come from a background of family business. In business departments, students from family businesses are estimated to make up as high as 40% of learners. The business owners may be good at marketing, sales, production, and operations, but many feel inadequate when it comes to reading financial statements and performing complex financial analysis to aid their decision making. As a result, family firm owner-managers rely on the accountant as one of their key advisors. Effective management of the business requires capable financial management and oversight. It would be ideal if a family member could provide these skills. This is another way for the succeeding generation to enter the family firm and add significant value to the business.

Many of the first-generation family business owners who are a part of the huge baby boom generation generation are retiring. They were a significantly entrepreneurial generation and started the majority of the businesses in the United States, many of which are family owned. This has fuelled a tremendous intergenerational transfer of wealth, as families attempt to have a successful succession or sell the family business. This provides a tremendous opportunity for professional service advisors, and it will create increased levels of change and risk for suppliers, who may have a large percentage of their customers with changes in ownership or management.

Family Foundations

Families in business are often philanthropic. As the family wealth grows, it eventually becomes advantageous to create a family foundation to channel the funds through and to provide ways to manage the requests, administer the funds, and assess the desired return on their social investment. Often, the family foundation stays in place long after the business has been sold. Some of the better-known and larger foundations are the Ford Family Foundation and The Rockefeller Foundation. Chick-fil-A founders Truett and Jeanette Cathy created the WinShape Foundation, and they channel their philanthropic efforts in education through college scholarships, summer camp experiences, and in foster care programs. A Cathy family member runs the foundation. The H. E. Butt Foundation is run by H. E. Butt Jr., the grandson of the founder of the Texas-based retail grocery chain that has been in business for over 100 years, with over $11 billion in sales.

Family Offices

One of the faster growing trends among family-owned businesses has been the creation of family offices. The business matures and becomes more complex, with several generations of ownership and multiple families involved, and as it grows and family members' wealth increases to significant amounts, the need emerges to have a professional family office to take care of the needs of the families. Usually the office is encouraged by the attorney, who becomes concerned about the amount of comingling of the family's needs with those of the business. Creation of a family office also becomes necessary when several groups of owners with varying amounts of shares, sometimes nonvoting, are involved. The need is also present when the family diversifies and becomes a group of family trusts, corporations, limited partnerships, or holding companies and has members with a variety of different investment vehicles. As the family business grows, its need for professional personal services grows. Family offices normally house the family foundation, and they are where the family often pools its wealth or investment funds for outside investments. Most often, these offices are operated by professional management.

Events such as an initial public offering, an acquisition, or a divesture may increase demands for professional services or cash. When a decision is made to sell the firm, family members often employ the family office as a way to hold the family together, maintain their leverage and power by investing as a group, access financial and legal services at no or low cost, and keep the family legacy alive. Family offices are dynamic and change as the family grows and transitions. Private wealth management and investment firms are now targeting the family office as a key customer.

A more advanced type of family office is a multifamily office (MFO). This is where several families may be under one family office. The Pitcairn family of the PPG fortune (Pittsburgh Plate Glass Company) sold their PPG holdings, and most of the 200-plus family members have stayed in business together through their Pitcairn Trust Company, a multifamily office that manages the Pitcairn family money, as well as those of other families and wealthy individuals. Through the professional wealth management professionals, the firm has been able to generate higher than average returns. The trust often invests in large publicly owned family businesses due to their long-term strategies and above-average financial results.

Family members who are not blood relatives but who are related to the family by marriage (family of attachment) are increasing: 14% of CEOs are related by marriage.[4] Another interesting trend is the increase of co-CEOs to lead the family firm. Approximately 9% of family firms have two CEOs, and 3.5% have three or more CEOs.[5] Co-CEO's are rarely seen in nonfamily firms. This shows another difference between family and nonfamily firms.

Nonfamily Management

In the early years of the business, when the firm is owned and managed by the founders, family members and perhaps a few key nonfamily employees operate the firm. When the firm has grown significantly, nonfamily management begins to play an increasingly important role. In later generations, such as a third- or fourth-generation firm, family members have retained ownership yet often outsource at least some of their management to professionals. Between 10% and 15% of family firms in the United States are now managed by nonfamily executives.[6] Family businesses have seen much success using a nonfamily member as an interim CEO, if a successor has not been identified or if the individual is not yet ready for the job. It can, however, be difficult to attract top-level managerial talent due to compensation issues such as stock options and the ability to pay competitive wages, compared to nonfamily firms. Most families have an aversion to issuing stock options, since this would effectively dilute family control.

Family firms have realized the need to attract highly effective and productive employees, developing mechanisms for motivation and fostering commitment, especially in smaller firms with several interested successors. In smaller family firms (usually the first and second generations), nonfamily employees have been frustrated by the amount of decision-making control exhibited by the family. There is a decision-making hierarchy: Nonfamily members are allowed to make smaller decisions in their areas of expertise, but family members usually make more important decisions.

Many family firms treat their employees better than nonfamily firms do. Employees feel they are appreciated more and have a more positive work experience at family-owned businesses. Many report feeling as if they are members of the family. This positive work environment is a tremendous source of competitive advantage. The president of a $3-million professional services firm states, "We have to be cautious of the impact to the company and our employees, since most of them have been here a long time. It's like they're family."[7]

Using Consultants

Another trend is the creation of specialized family business consultants. Twenty years ago, the consultants were primarily former family business owners who had awareness of the issues or accountants and lawyers who had experience with family firms. With the increase in the awareness and importance of family business, with its unique differences and complexities, specialized consultants now offer a wide array of services to family firms. Usually, a generalist consultant is familiar with the family business issues of conflict, succession, and strategic planning. Following the initial meeting and an assessment of the firm, the consultant generally brings in other types of specialists to deal with specific issues. For example, family counselors are used to deal with serious interpersonal conflict. There are practices and techniques of a specialized nature that can only be used by a qualified counselor. The positive impact on the family and the business can be quite dramatic and very effective. When the situation deems, lawyers, valuation specialists, accountants, tax and estate planning specialists, business brokers, or insurance brokers may all be called.

However, family members often show a significant amount of reticence to utilize the services of a consultant. This is especially true among the first-generation family firms, who often have a paternalistic and authoritarian style of management. This inhibition is due to privacy concerns, a lack of awareness concerning how the issues are affecting other family members, and the expense of consultants.

Future Research

Because the academic study of family business is a relatively recent activity, much research work remains to provide better help and resources to family firms, as well as to separate general management type of advice from the specific and particular advice needed to effectively operate a family-owned firm. The most pressing need in family business research is to arrive at an agreed definition of a family business. Then, when researchers carry out studies, the criteria for entrance into the study will be similar and comparable. There is a significant difference between a large business (e.g., Ford or Wal-Mart) and the much more common variety (e.g., small family-owned dry cleaners or local hardware stores). A uniform definition would enable comparison of apples to apples, instead of apples to oranges. The benefit will be more accurate and useful information to practitioners who consult with family firms and to the family firms themselves in the form of recommendations and best practices. A generally agreed-on definition of family business would allow researchers to study important issues and arrive at conclusions with some *finality*, such as studying the financial performance of family firms and comparing them with nonfamily firms.

Since the domain of family business research is relatively recent, there is considerable research needed in many more areas. Succession has been well studied, yet there are numerous significant topics that have not been studied in a well-controlled and scholarly manner. Much of the early research in the area was conducted as single case studies and often by consultants. Understudied areas include governance, wealth management, the family office, and the intersection of family firms and entrepreneurship.

Good research requires asking the right questions and designing the proper study with a correct utilization of the full menu of research methodologies (both qualitative and quantitative) in order to arrive at generalizable research. The research domain would benefit from the full spectrum of research methods, including empirical research.

The domain would also benefit by being more interdisciplinary. Great advances in knowledge often happen when we expand our research to other fields of study. Most of what is published in family business research has been in business/management and entrepreneurship. For example, a small amount of historians have researched the history of family business and made a beneficial impact. It would be helpful to work with psychologists, sociologists, anthropologists, economists, family studies, and finance and accounting scholars.

Decision Making

If family business members have a better understanding of their own decision-making abilities (or lack thereof) and understand the barriers they face in decision making, the potential exists for improvement in decision-making effectiveness. Decision making is another of the major areas of opportunity for family-owned businesses, along with instituting a board and creating a strategic plan.

Studying the Generations

It will be beneficial for future researchers, practitioners, and family businesses themselves to have a better understanding of the differences among the generations involved in a family business. Each generation makes decisions differently based on their unique goals and objectives. More research should be performed in this area, as a second-generation firm is seen to be different from a first-generation firm or a third-generation firm. As an example, it is vitally important to study the second-generation population because of its prevalence within the family business, the low succession rate from the first generation to the second generation, and the even lower succession rate from the second generation to the third generation. According to Ernst & Young consulting, almost three quarters of family businesses in the Middle East are owned and managed by the second generation and one-fifth are third generation. This is good news for family firms everywhere. More study needs to be done to uncover what the Middle East families are doing to account for the higher rates of intergenerational succession.[8]

Co-CEOs

Co-chief executive officers (co-CEOs) are family business leaders who share the responsibility and leadership of the firm with one other member. According to the American Family Business Survey,[9] an arrangement such as this has become more common in family businesses, with 12.5% of survey respondents reporting co-CEOs. A significant proportion (35.1%) of respondents forecasted that they would have co-CEOs in the next generation. This type of responsibility and power-sharing role is practically unheard of in nonfamily firms. This may be an excellent way to enable a successful succession, foster teamwork, and avoid the loss of any key family members who may have not been chosen for the top job. A close relation to co-CEOs is the concept of a copreneur, which is a (usually married) couple who founded and manages a business together.

Some family firms, when faced with equally qualified candidates for leadership, have instituted a creative solution: a revolving office that may last for a year or two in which the family members revolve in and out of the CEO position. This arrangement has not been well studied by academics; most information is self-reported or anecdotal in nature. However, if workable, it can be an excellent way to avoid family conflict and to prevent family members from leaving the firm.

Conclusion

The family business is the lifeblood of our global economy. This has been true throughout history and continues to be true today. The vast majority of firms are family owned, and they account for a significant percentage of most countries' gross domestic product. Very importantly, they employ the majority of workers and account for the highest percentage of all new jobs. Family-owned firms are the pillars in our communities and our business society.

This book was written to introduce the reader to the importance of family-owned businesses to provide some evidence of their importance and to make the case that family-owned businesses are separate and unique compared with nonfamily businesses. When a family business owner or top manager reads a business magazine or watches a television show on a financial news channel, do they see themselves being discussed? Are they able to relate to a *Fortune* 500 nonfamily firm? Are they able to benefit from the work of many business academics and apply the newly presented concepts and theories to increasing the effectiveness and profitability of their family firm? The answer is, most often, no.

Family business owners, employees, and family members—you are different! You have specific issues, problems, and most importantly, *opportunities* that nonfamily firms do not have. As the academic community increasingly realizes that you are different, they will do a better job of providing you with helpful information in the form of specific research, tools, and techniques for family firms.

It is hoped readers gain a more complete understanding of the complex nature of family businesses and have a deeper appreciation for the challenges and struggles of family firms. It is also hoped that a family business owner will feel more pride as to the contribution they make to our society. These firms should be celebrated, not derided. A family firm that has succeeded for two to three generations, or longer, is worthy of our esteem. More than likely, their nonfamily competitors already give them considerable respect in the marketplace

APPENDIX A

Selected Further Reading

This book has benefited from the work of several family business scholars who wrote excellent review articles and books. The following is not an exhaustive list covering all family business research; however, by reviewing the following, readers seeking more information on family businesses can find a significant amount of information.

Books

- Danny Miller and Isabelle Le Breton-Miller's *Managing for the Long Run: Lessons in Competitive Advantage From Great Family Businesses* (2005). This book is an excellent example of the positives of family businesses. By studying excellent family businesses, many of them over 100 years old, the authors were able to define what the excellent companies did that made them so much more successful than their nonfamily competitors.
- Ernesto Poza wrote the definitive textbook on family business. Simply titled *Family Business* (2013), it is now in its fourth edition. The book is used by many university-based family business centers and by professors teaching family business courses. Professor Poza has created case studies for students or family business members to work on together.
- Gregg McCann is the author of *When Your Parents Sign Your Paycheck: Finding Career Success Inside or Outside the Family Business* (2007). The book is an excellent tool for the future generations of a family business to evaluate who they are as a person, their goals and objectives, and whether or not they should enter the family business.
- Kelin E. Gersick, John A. Davis, Marion McCallom Hampton, and Ican Lansberg wrote *Generation to Generation: Life Cycles*

of the Family Business (1997). A classic within family business studies, this book is an excellent read to help understand
the various problems and issues associated with the different
generations and stages of the family business.

- *Keeping the Family Business Healthy* (1987) by John Ward is
  a family business classic from one of the pioneers in family
  business research.
- *Cultural Change in Family Firms* (1986) by W. Gibb Dyer Jr. is
  another classic from another family business pioneer.
- *Working With the Ones You Love* (1990) by Dennis Jaffe was
  written from a family therapy perspective.
- *Perpetuating the Family Business: 50 Lessons Learned From Long-
  Lasting Successful Families in Business* (2004) by John Ward is
  an excellent book full of pearls of wisdom.
- *Entrepreneurial Family Firms* (2010) by Frank Hoy and
  Pramodita Sharma presents the entrepreneurial nature of
  family businesses from start-up to growth and maturity.
  Discussion questions and learning exercises are included.
- *The History of Family Firms* (2003) by Andrea Colli provides
  an excellent overview of the history of family business internationally from 1850 to 2000.
- *Dynasties: Fortunes and Misfortunes of the World's Greatest
  Family Businesses* (2006) was written by a historian and economics professor but for a general audience. David Landes
  presents fascinating information on well-known family firms
  throughout history such as the Rothschilds, the Morgans,
  the Rockefellers, the Guggenheims, the Shlumbergers, Ford,
  Agnelli, and others.
- *Family Wars* (2008) by Grant Gordon and Nigel Nicholson is
  an entertaining and often salacious book concerning 24 well-
  known family businesses and their conflicts.
- *Beer Wars* (2016) by Frances Stroh chronicles her life as a
  fourth generation family member of the Stroh Beer Company.
  At one time listed as one of the richest families in the country,
  it is a tale of poor succession and bad decision making.
- In the style of *Family Wars*, *The House of Mondavi: The Rise
  and Fall of an American Wine Dynasty* (2007) by Julia Flynn

Siler chronicles the history of the pioneering family of the Napa Valley wine industry. It reads like a novel and will give anyone pause about going public, even when the family has kept majority control of the stock.

- *Handbook of Research on Family Business* (2006), edited by Panikkos Zata Poutziouris, Kosmas X. Smyrnios, and Sabine B. Klein, contains 33 chapters written by different authors who are all academics in family business.
- *Handbook of Research on Family Business, Second Edition* (2013), edited by Kosmas Smyrnios, Panikkos Zata Poutziouris, and Sanjay Goel.
- *The Sage Handbook of Family Business.* (2014), edited by Leif Melin, Mattias Nordqvist, and Pramadita Sharma. This book has 35 chapters written by family business scholars.

Magazines

- *Family Business Magazine* is the only publication specifically targeted for family business owners. Published quarterly, its articles and columns answer everyday issues and problems for family firms. Success tips of family firms are also discussed. Every year it profiles the oldest family businesses, as well as the largest family businesses in the world. Family business research is summarized and made applicable for families to utilize in their own business. Published for over 20 years, it is a valuable resource for family business owners and the consultants who service them.
- *Tharawat Magazine* is targeted for the specific issues and opportunities of Arabian family businesses in the Middle East as well as internationally.

Journals

By far, the number one academic journal within the family business area is the *Family Business Review* published by the Family Firm Institute. The second journal in order of number of published family business studies is *Entrepreneurial Theory and Practice*, followed by the *Journal of Business*

Venturing and the *Journal of Small Business Management.* These journals account for the vast majority of all peer-reviewed family business articles. Recently, two new journals specifically focusing on family business were created: *The Journal of Family Business Strategy* and the *Journal of Family Business Management* (launched in 2011). These new journals attest to the increasing interest of business researchers and the importance of family business.

APPENDIX B
Family Business Resources

The Family Firm Institute (FFI)
 The FFI is the premiere international body for research and advising in the family business and family wealth fields.

The International Family Enterprise Research Academy (IFERA)
 The IFERA is devoted to research, theory, and practice of family business with an emphasis on scholarship.

The Family Business Network (FBN)
 The FBN is a not-for-profit international network operated by family businesses, for family businesses, with the goal of strengthening family business success over generations. They have thousands of family business members all over the world.

Family Enterprise USA (FEUSA)
 FEUSA is a membership advocacy group whose primary purpose is to increase public awareness of the importance of family business.

United States Association of Small Business
and Entrepreneurship (USASBE)
 The USASBE includes a family business special interest group within this organization, the largest entrepreneurial association in the United States.

The Institute for Family Business (IFB)
 The IFB is an independent nonprofit organization that supports family business in the United Kingdom through research, education, and policy advocacy (see http://www.ifb.org.uk).

Tharawat Family Business Forum
 The Tharawat Family Business Forum is an Arab family business network established in 2007. It publishes *Tharawat Magazine*.

APPENDIX C

Glossary

altruism: Unselfish concern for the welfare of others at the expense of oneself, for example, when families make business decisions that actually hurt the business, such as avoiding layoffs in a downturn or keeping a long-term yet unproductive employee.

birth order: The order of birth in a specific family from first to last, such as oldest, middle, and youngest. Each position has different characteristics and plays a different role within the family.

board of advisors: A semiformal group of business advisors charged with making suggestions and nonbinding recommendations to the firm.

board of directors: The formal organization required for all corporations that has authority, responsibility, and decision-making power. In family firms, these roles are usually held by family members, with few outside (nonfamily) members.

conflict: Conflict means to be in serious and direct opposition with another's ideas, viewpoints, plans, and strategy. Conflict can often be very contentious to the point of violent disagreement. When this occurs interpersonally, especially among family members, it has a negative impact on the family business. Intersibling rivalry can erupt into full-blown conflict. Conversely, conflict can be positive if all sides are able to share freely, and debate over the process of how work should be done (called task conflict). In this manner, good decisions can be made, and work is performed efficiently.

copreneurs: A couple who owns a business together.

cousin consortium: Usually the third generation, they are the children of the sons and daughters of the founders and they form a larger group than either the first generation or the second generation.

culture: This is a company's unique set of values, norms, beliefs, history, and experiences, which make up the unique character of the organization. In a family business with a "positive" culture, the family members and employees have a shared system of beliefs, attitudes, and norms of behavior. It can be a source of tremendous competitive advantage. Conversely, in a business with a "negative" organizational culture, the employees do not share a similar value system, owners and managers may be at odds with employees, and there are no norms to guide decisions.

entrepreneur: Defined as the original founder of the organization; in a family business, an entrepreneur is synonymous with the first-generation founder of the business.

entrepreneurial family business: A family business that retains the original entrepreneurial spirit of the founder.

entrepreneurship: There are numerous definitions of entrepreneurship. Most researchers can agree entrepreneurship is the creation of something new that did not exist before and has some level of associated risk.

estate planning: The proactive discussion and planning for a person's disposition of property, possessions, and capital. It is usually purposefully and proactively structured to minimize taxes and maximize generational wealth.

explicit knowledge: This type of knowledge is clear and obvious. It is gained by education and reading and expressed by words, numbers, and codes. It is the opposite of tacit knowledge.

familiness: A term created to describe the interplay between the family and the business, it includes the various forms of capital, such as human, social, financial, and physical, that are unique to the family business.

family: Most commonly refers to a nuclear family of blood relatives, such as a father, a mother, and their offspring. In family business terms, it can refer to extended family members and in-laws. The individuals are committed to mutual growth and development. They share a family history together and have strong bonds.

family business: There is not one well-accepted definition of family business. The most common definition is where the family, consisting of more than one family member, owns a significant amount of the firm and influences the strategy of the business.

family constitution: A formal document stating the firm's mission, vision, and purpose. It is also used to outline policies and procedures for the family in the business.

family control: This is used when discussing large companies, often with outside shareholders. The family may have enough ownership to exercise a high level of input on the strategic direction of the firm.

family council: A semiformal council made up of family members. The purpose of the council is to have a proper venue for airing and discussing business and family issues. Usually items are presented, discussed, and voted on.

family foundation: The philanthropic (charitable) arm of the family.

family meeting: A very informal meeting of the family members used to increase communication and disseminate company information.

family of attachment: This refers to those who have entered the family by other methods than blood, such by as marriage.

family office: A group of service professionals who manage the family wealth, as well as provide accountancy and legal services, specifically for the family. Usually the family charitable foundations are housed in the family office.

family of origin: This is your blood family from birth.

family roles: Familial roles are generally assigned to us early in life. For example, the youngest member of the family is the baby, the older child has extra responsibilities, and there may be the black sheep of the family. It can be difficult for other family members to see the person as anything different.

gazelles: A term used to describe fast-growing family firms.

genogram: A diagram that lists the family lineage as far back as can be traced. Items include marriages, deaths, diseases, divorces, business ownership, entrepreneurship, and other pertinent facts.

governance: The formal measures of control instituted for effective management of the firm. Governance items include boards of directors, the family constitution, human resource policies, and similar items.

human capital: A measure of the economic value of the employee or employees.

individual life cycle: Each person goes through a cycle of birth, adolescence, teens, young adult, adulthood, later adulthood, and finally, death.

legacy: What the founder leaves behind. In the case of a family business, this may be a successful firm and the norms, mission, and vision handed down through the generations.

life cycle: The stages of development. The complete processes of change and development of individuals, products, and organizations.

management: The administration, organization, and control of the business. Proper management is necessary for success.

mission: A statement that defines the purpose, duty, objective, or task of the family business.

nepotism: Preferential treatment of family members in regard to employment, promotions, and compensation.

organizational life cycle: An organization also has a series of life cycles. But unlike an individual, the organization can live forever.

paternalistic management style: This means managing or governing the business, employees, and family members, as a father that is often dictatorial but in a loving way. A person with this management style habitually does not allow people to exercise their free will.

patient capital: As investment funds garnered by family members and friends, the funds have a longer-term outlook than other sources of capital.

personality: Characteristics, attitudes, emotional responses, behavioral patterns, social roles, and traits people display to others.

primogeniture: Referred to as the "right" of male primogeniture in many cultures, this is the long-standing norm of the first-born son to take over the family business.

product life cycle: The product life cycle goes through four distinct stages: introduction, growth, maturity, and decline. Decisions for business optimization are made at each stage.

pruning the family tree: To avoid having too many family employees or to keep the business in only one branch of the family, other family members may be bought out or encouraged to start a separate business.

shareholder council: Similar to a board, it is an organization of the shareholders of the business. Meetings are held for family members to discuss issues and make decisions.

sibling partnership: This describes a partnership of siblings, usually the second-generation children of the founders.

sibling rivalry: As the children grow, they may engage in competitive or aggressive behavior out of attention for parental love and affection. This behavior can exhibit itself when siblings try to break out of their family roles, with the conflict becoming problematic in the family firm.

social capital: The resources (e.g., ideas, information, money, and trust) that an individual is able to access through a social network. A high level of earned social capital is thought to be one reason behind a family firm's competitive advantage.

social network: A social structure consisting of individuals or organizations connected by ties such as a relationship, link, or bond.

socioemotional wealth: A popular family business theory which discusses the importance of the emotional component within the family. The family gets value from their ownership of the firm in more ways than just monetary. Family pride, and their standing in the community are important factors.

stakeholder: Those who have an interest or stake in the firm or who can be affected by the business, such as customers, employees, and shareholders.

strategic planning: A process used to define the company objectives, assess internal and external situations, formulate a strategy, implement the strategy, evaluate the strategy, and make necessary adjustments.

succession: The transfer of ownership or leadership from one generation to another. This is likely the most problematic issue in a family business.

system: A combination of related individual parts organized into a whole. A family business is a complex system consisting of three subsystems: the family, the business, and the management of the business.

tacit knowledge: This type of knowledge is gained by being with and around other people; it is a sum of experiences. It requires joint or shared activities to develop. It is implicit, unspoken, and gained by observation. It is the opposite of explicit knowledge.

trust: In family businesses, trust is a critical component and is necessary in the creation of a competitive advantage. Agency costs are reduced due to high levels of trust. Conversely, when a family is low on trust, dysfunction results.

values: The principles, standards, and norms to which the business aspires. In a family business, the values are accepted by the group and are often passed down to the successive generations.

vision: The long-term goals of the family business, usually expressed in a vision statement.

Family Business Checklist

Questions for the Family

1. Do we have a valid business plan?
2. Do we have a mission statement?
3. Are our company values clear?
4. Do we have a strategic plan for the business?
5. Do we have a family business constitution?
6. How will we make decisions? Who will make decisions?
7. Does the business have specific sales and profit goals?
8. Are the family business goals agreed on by the family?
9. How do family members feel about selling the business outside of the family?
10. Should we work with consultants? Under what circumstances?
11. Is there a fair compensation and reward system for family as well as nonfamily members?
12. Is the compensation system based on market value?
13. Is there an employee performance appraisal system?
14. Who should evaluate family employees?
15. Do we have nonfamily managers, and do we encourage them?
16. What are the rights and responsibilities of nonfamily employees?
17. Are there policies for family members to join or exit the business?
18. Should the next generation be required to obtain a university education before entry into the firm?
19. Should the next generation be required to have some outside work experience before entry into the firm? If so, how much?
20. Do we have written hiring and firing policies and procedures?
21. Do we have written job descriptions?
22. Should a board of advisors or directors be instituted?
23. Should we start a family council?
24. Are our sales increasing?

25. Is the industry outlook positive?
26. Is the industry highly competitive?
27. Is the business financially healthy?
28. Is the next generation interested in the business?
29. Are all family members welcome to join the firm?
30. Is there a succession plan?
31. Is a system for successor development in place?
32. Are women treated equally in the business?
33. Are there avenues in place to increase family communication?
34. Is there a significant amount of interpersonal conflict? Sibling rivalry?
35. Is there a conflict management and resolution system?
36. How does the family feel about selling shares to the public?
37. What role does debt play in the firm? How much or how little?
38. How much risk do we feel comfortable having?

Questions for the Next Generation

1. Is it your intention to enter the family firm?
2. Why do you want to join the firm?
3. Do you have necessary experience and education?
4. What are your strengths and skills that can aid the company?
5. Are you willing to make sacrifices for the firm, such as receive low pay or work long hours when necessary?
6. What is your long-term vision for the company?
7. Are your values in line with the founder's values and the company's stated mission?
8. Have you gained any outside work experience?
9. Do you feel pressured to be the successor? Is it your choice?
10. Do you believe the business should stay in the family?

There are numerous questions, and these would require a significant amount of time and attention in order to answer. The families who have successfully managed intergenerational successions and moved to more professional levels of management have successfully worked through many of these questions.

Notes

Introduction

1. See Poza (2007), p. 1.
2. Overview (2008).
3. See Collins and Porras (2004).
4. Kachner, Stalk, and Bloch (2012).
5. Drucker (1994).
6. Alderson (2011).
7. *Forbes* (2009), p. 22.
8. Schroeder (1998).

Chapter 1

1. Chandler (1990).
2. Sharma et al. (1996).
3. Colli et al. (2003), p. 30.
4. Miller and Le Breton-Miller (2003), p. 127.
5. Chua et al. (1999).
6. Poza (2007), p. 4.
7. Astrachan and Shanker (2003).
8. Astrachan and Shanker (2003), p. 216.

Chapter 2

1. See Miller and Le Breton-Miller (2005b).
2. SC Johnson (n.d.).
3. Chick-fil-A (n.d.).
4. Enterprise Holdings (n.d.).
5. Friedman (1970).
6. Freeman (1984).
7. MassMutual Financial Group/Raymond Institute (2002).
8. Laird Norton Tyee (2007).
9. Laird Norton Tyee (2007).
10. Emling (2000), pp. 67–68.
11. See Dyer (1986); Ibrahim et al. (2008).
12. History of the Hénokiens (n.d.).

13. Wallop (2013).
14. Edelman Trust Barometer (2017).
15. Edelman (2017).
16. MassMutual Financial Group/Raymond Institute (2002).
17. See Miller and Le Breton-Miller (2005b).
18. See McConaughy et al. (2001).
19. Lee (2006a).
20. See Anderson and Reeb (2003).
21. See Miller and Le Breton-Miller (2005).
22. Ibrahim et al. (2008), p. 95.
23. Kachner, Stalk, and Bloch (2012).
24. Le Breton-Miller and Miller (2015).
25. Revilla et al. (2016).
26. Pindado and Requej (2015).
27. MassMutual Financial Group (2007).
28. See Alderson (2009).
29. See Alderson (2009).
30. See Upton and Felan (2001).
31. Breeze (2009).
32. Niehm et al. (2008).
33. SC Johnson (n.d.).
34. See Sharma and Irving (2005).
35. Aronoff and Ward (1998), p. 98.
36. Edelman (2017).
37. Edelman (2017).
38. Susanto and Susanto (2013)
39. Sirmon and Hitt (2003).
40. Miller, Steier, and Le Breton Miller (2016).
41. PWC (2015).
42. See Neal and Veal (2008).

Chapter 3

1. See Tagiuri and Davis (1996).
2. Poza (2007), p. 4.
3. See Habershon et al. (2003).
4. See Chrisman et al. (2003); Sirmon and Hitt (2003).
5. Chrisman et al. (2003), p. 21.
6. See Chrisman et al. (2003); Habershon et al. (2003).
7. See Mustakallio et al. (2002).
8. Gomez-Mejia et al. (2007); Gomez-Mejia et al. (2011).

9. Berrone et al. (2012).
10. See Sharma (2004).

Chapter 4

1. See Aronoff and Astrachan (1996).
2. See Aronoff and Astrachan (1996).
3. See Sonfield and Lussier (2004).
4. See Feltham et al. (2005).
5. See Aronoff and Astrachan (1996).
6. See Welsch (1996).
7. Ibrahim et al. (2008).
8. See Prince and File (1995).
9. See Miller and Le Breton-Miller (2005b).
10. See Miller and Le Breton-Miller (2005b).
11. Miller and Le Breton-Miller (2005b), p. 11.
12. See Prince and File (1995; 1996).
13. See File (2005).
14. See File (2005).
15. See Sharma and Manikutty (2005).
16. See Goffe and Scase (1985).
17. Carney (2005), p. 58.
18. Carney (2005), p. 66.
19. Carney (2005), p. 63.
20. Carney (2005), p. 249.
21. Carney (2005), p. 251.
22. Poza (2009), p. 15.
23. Kets de Vries (1993), p. 63.
24. Welsh (1996).
25. See Agor (1989); Harris and Ogbana (2005); Kakkonen (2005).
26. See Alderson (2009).
27. See Alderson (2009).
28. See Alderson (2009).
29. See Alderson (2009).
30. See Aronoff and Astrachan (1996).

Chapter 5

1. See Alderson (2009).
2. See Ward (2004).

3. See Levinson (1971).
4. See Hilburt-Davis and Dyer (2003); Poza (2007).
5. See PricewaterhouseCoopers (2007/2008).
6. See Alderson (2009).
7. See Alderson (2009).
8. See Alderson (2009).
9. See MassMutual Financial Group/Raymond Institute (2002).
10. See American Family Business Survey (2009).
11. KPMG (2009).
12. Kelly et al. (2000), p. 27.
13. Davis and Harveston (1998), p. 311.
14. See Alderson (2009).
15. See Alderson (2009).
16. See Alderson (2009).
17. See Alderson (2009).
18. Aronoff et al. (1997), p. 1.
19. Gersick et al. (1997), p. 171.

Chapter 6

1. See Ward (1986).
2. See Poza (2009).
3. See MassMutual Financial Group/Raymond Institute (2002).
4. See Laird Norton Tyee (2007).
5. See Dascher and Jens (1999).
6. See MassMutual Financial Group/Raymond Institute (2002).
7. See Birley (1986).
8. See MassMutual Financial Group/Raymond Institute (2002).
9. Stavrou (1999).
10. Adapted from Grant Thornton International (n.d.).
11. See MassMutual Financial Group/Raymond Institute (2002).
12. Shearman & Sterling, LLC (2017).
13. See Leach and Bogood (1999).
14. See Pearl (2010).

Chapter 7

1. See Gersick et al. (1997).
2. Poza (2007), pp. 8–10.
3. Bianchi and Alderson (2011).
4. MassMutual Financial Group/Raymond Institute (2002).

Chapter 8

1. See Miller and Le Breton-Miller (2005a).
2. Fairlie and Robb (2007).
3. Stwart and Hitt (2012).
4. Family Business Confidence Survey (2013).
5. PWC (2015).
6. Edelman (2017).
7. Family business (2007).

Chapter 9

1. Vera and Dean (2005).
2. EY (2015).
3. Picchi (2017).
4. MassMutual Financial Group/Raymond Institute (2002).
5. MassMutual Financial Group/Raymond Institute (2002).
6. Family business (2007).
7. See Alderson (2009).
8. Arabic Knowledge@Wharton (2010).
9. MassMutual Financial Group/Raymond Institute (2002).

References

Agor, W. H. (1989). Intuition in organizations. In W. H. Agor (Ed.), *Intuition in organizations*, p. 288. Newbury Park, CA: Sage.

Alderson, K. (2011). *An analysis of the family business wealth from the Forbes 400.* Unpublished manuscript.

Alderson, K. (2009). *Exploring the complexities of family business decision making: How the second generation makes decisions.* PhD dissertation, School of Business and Technology Capella University, Minneapolis, MN.

Aminoff, P., Karsma, K., & Elo-Parssinen, K. (2006, July). *Family entrepreneurship: Family enterprises as the engines of continuity, renewal and growth-intensiveness.* Helsinki, Finland: Finnish Ministry of Trade and Industry. Retrieved from http://perheyritystenliitto.fi/files/FINFamilyBusinessReport_2006_English .pdf

Amit, R., Ding, Y., Villalonga, B., & Zhang, H. (2010). The role of institutional development in the prevalence and value of family firms. Harvard Business School Working Paper. Retrieved from http://www.hbs.edu/research/pdf/10 -103.pdf

Anderson, R. C., & Reeb, D. M. (2003). Founding family ownership and firm performance: Evidence from the S&P 500. *The Journal of Finance, 63,* 1301–1328.

Arabic Knowledge@Wharton. (2010, March 8). Family firms in the Middle East: The new rules of engagement. Retrieved from http://knowledge.wharton .upenn.edu/arabic/article.cfm?articleid=2405

Astrachan, J. H., & Shanker, M. C. (2003). Family businesses' contribution to the U.S. economy: A closer look. *Family Business Review, 16,* 211–219.

Aronoff, C. E., & Ward, J. L. (1998). Why continue your family's business? *Nations Business, 86*(3), 72–74.

Aronoff, C. E., Astrachan, J. H., Mendoza, D. S., & Ward, J. L. (1997). *Making sibling teams work.* Marietta, GA: Family Enterprise.

Aronoff, C. E., & Astrachan, J. H. (1996). How to make better decisions. *Nations Business, 84*(1), 39.

Barclays Wealth. (2007). Family businesses: In safe hands? *Barclays Wealth Insights, 8.* Retrieved from http://www.barclayswealth.com/insights/library.htm

Bianchi, C., & Alderson, K. (2011). *Family council effectiveness: Interviews with families, consultants, and academics.* Unpublished manuscript.

Birdthistle, N., & Fleming, P. (2007). Under the microscope: A profile of the family business in Ireland. *Irish Journal of Management: Special Edition on Entrepreneurship, 28*(2), 133–168.

Blumentritt, T. P., Keyt, A. D., & Astrachan, J. H. (2007). Creating an environment for successful nonfamily CEOs: An exploratory study of good principles. *Family Business Review, 20,* 321–355.

Berdugo, E., & Cáceres, L. S. (2010). Aproximación al estado de la investigación en empresas de familia en Colombia: 1989–2009. *Gestión & Sociedad, 2*(2), 134–157.

Berrone, P., Cruz, C., & Gomez-Mejia, L. R. (2012). Socioemotional wealth in family firms: Theoretical dimensions, assessment approaches, and agenda for future research. *Family Business Review, 25*(3). 258–279.

Birley, S., (2001). Owner manager attitudes to family and business issues: A 16 country study. *Entrepreneurship Theory and Practice, 26*(2), 63–76.

Bowman-Upton, N. (1991). *Transferring management in the family owned business.* Washington DC: U.S. Small Business Association.

Breeze, B. (2009). *Natural philanthropists: findings of the family business philanthropy and social responsibility inquiry.* Project report. Institute for Family Business (University of Kent, UK). Retrieved from https://kar.kent.ac.uk/37241/

Carney, M. (2005). Corporate governance and competitive advantage in family controlled firms. *Entrepreneurship Theory and Practice, 29,* 249–265.

Casillas, J., & Acedo, F. (2007). Evolution of the intellectual structure of family business literature: A bibliometric study of FBR. *Family Business Review, 20,* 2.

Chandler, A. D. (1990) *Scale and scope: The dynamics of industrial capitalism.* Cambridge, MA: Belknap Press.

Chick-fil-A. (n.d.). Chick-fil-A website. Retrieved from http://www.chick-fil-a.com/#story

Chrisman, J. J., Chua, J. H., & Steier, L. (2005). Sources and consequences of distinctive familiness: An introduction. *Entrepreneurship Theory and Practice, 29,* 237–247.

Chrisman, J., Chua, J., & Sharma, P. (2003). *Current trends and future directions in family business management studies: Toward a theory of the family firm.* (Coleman White Paper Series). Kent, OH: Coleman Foundation and U.S. Association of Small Business and Entrepreneurship.

Chrisman, J. J., Kellermanns, F. W., Chan, K. C., & Liano, K. (2010, March 23). Intellectual foundations of current research in family business: An identification and review of 25 influential articles. *Family Business Review,* 9–26.

Chua, J. H., Chrisman, J. J., & Sharma, P. (1999, summer). Defining the family business by behavior. *Entrepreneurship Theory and Practice,* 19–39.

Colli, A., Fernandez-Perez, P., & Rose, M. (2003). National determinants of family firm development: Family firms in Britain, Spain and Italy in the 19th and 20th centuries. *Enterprise and Society, 4*(1), 28–65.

Collins, J. C., & Porras, J. I. (1994). *Built to last: Successful habits of visionary companies.* New York, NY: HarperCollins.

CS Family 1000. (2017). Credit Suiss Research Institute. Retrieved from https://credit-suisse.com/corporate/en/research/research-institute/publications.html

Dascher, P. E., & Jens, W. G. (1999). Family business succession planning, executive briefing. *Business Horizons, 42*(5), 2–4.

Davis, P. S., & Harveston, P. D. (2001). The phenomenon of conflict in the family firm: A cross generational study. *Journal of Small Business Management, 39*(1), 14–30.

Davis, P. S., & Harveston, P. D. (1998). The influence of family on the family business succession process: A multi-generational perspective. *Entrepreneurship Theory and Practice, 22*(3), 31–53.

Drucker, P. F. (1994, August 19). How to save the family business. *The Wall Street Journal.*

Dyer, W. G., Jr. (2006). Examining the "family effect" on firm performance. *Family Business Review, 19*, 253–273.

Dyer, W. G., Jr. (1988). Culture and continuity in family firms. *Family Business Review, 1*, 37–50.

Dyer, W. G., Jr. (1986). *Cultural change in family firms: Anticipating and managing business and family transitions.* San Francisco, CA: Jossey-Bass.

Edelman Trust Barometer (2017). Special Report: Family Business. Retrieved from https://edelman.com/trust2017/family-business-trust/

Eddleston, K. A., Otondo, R. F., & Kellermanns, F. W. (2008). Conflict, participative decision-making, and generational ownership dispersion: A multilevel analysis. *Journal of Small Business Management, 46*, 456–484.

Edelman (2017). *The edelman trust barometer 2017.* Special Report: Family Business. Retrieved from https://edelman.com/trust2017/family-business-trust/

Eisenhardt, K., Kahwajy, J., & Bourgeois, L. (1997). How management teams can have a good fight. *Harvard Business Review, 77*–85.

Emling, E. (2000). *Svenskt familjeföretagande* (Licentiate thesis, Economic Research Institute, Stockholm School of Economics, Stockholm, Sweden).

Enterprise Holdings. (n.d.). Enterprise Holdings corporate website. Retrieved from http://www.enterpriseholdings.com/about_us/heritage.html

EY (2015). Women in leadership: The family business advantage. *Ernst & Young.* Retrieved from http://ey.com/Publication/vwLUAssets/ey-women-in-leadership-the-family-business-advantage/$FILE/ey-women-in-leadership-the-family-business-advantage.pdf

Family Firm Institute. (n.d.). Facts and figures: United States. Retrieved from http://www.ffi.org

Fairlie, R. W., & Robb, A. (2007). Families, human capital, and small business: Evidence from the characteristics of business owner's survey. *Industrial and Labor Relations Review, 60*(2), 225–245.

Family Businesses. (2003). Family businesses dominate: International Family Enterprise Research Academy (IFERA). *Family Business Review, 16*(4), 235–240.

Family Business Confidence Survey (2013). Elizabethtown College, Pennsylvania. Retrieved from https://etown.edu/depts/business/files/events/474%20Family%20Business%20Confidence%20Survey-Single%20Pages.pdf

Family Business in Ireland. (2008). *Family business in Ireland, services sectors 2005.* Dublin, Ireland: Central Statistics Office, Government of Ireland. Retrieved from http://www.cso.ie/releasespublications/documents/services/2005/fbi 2005.pdf

Family Firms Institute. (n.d.). Global data points. Retrieved from http://www.ffi.org/default.asp?id=398

FBN International. (2007). Family business international monitor. Retrieved from http://www.fbn-i.org/fbn/web.nsf/ArticlesLU/AA3786AA36C250F98 72575210070073E?OpenDocument

Feltham, T. S., Feltham, G., & Barnett, J. J. (2005). The dependence of family businesses on a single decision maker. *Journal of Small Business Management, 43*(1), 1–15.

File, K. (2005). *Professor studies how family businesses make decisions.* Storrs, CT: University of Connecticut School of Business Administration, Family Business Program. Retrieved from http://www.fambiz.com

Freeman, R. E. (1984). Strategic management: A stakeholder approach. The Pitman Series in Business and Public Policy. Harper Collins College Division, NY.

Friedman, M. (1970, September 13). The social responsibility of business is to increase its profits. *New York Times Magazine,* 2.

Forbes. (2009, October 11). The *Forbes* 400 richest Americans 2009. *Forbes, 186*(6), 22.

Gersick, K. E., Davis, J. A., Hampton, M. M., & Lansberg, I. (1997). *Generation to generation: Life cycles of the family business.* Boston, MA: Harvard Business School Press.

Gersick, K. E., Lansberg, I., Desjardins, M., & Dunn, B. (1999). Staging and transitions: Managing change in the family business. *Family Business Review, 12,* 287–297.

Goto, T. (2005). Family business no genjo to kadai [Perspectives and issues of family business]. *Bulletin of Shizuoka Sangyo University, 7,* 225–337.

Goffe, R., & Scase, R. (1985). Proprietal control in family firms: Some functions of "quasi-organic" management systems. *Journal of Management Studies, 22,* 53–68.

Gomez-Mejia, L. R., Nunez-Nickel, M., & Guttierez, I. (2001). The role of family ties in agency contracts. *Academy of Management Journal, 44*(1), 1–95.

Gomez-Mejia, L. R., Haynes, K., Nunez-Nickel, M., Jacobson, K. J., & Mayonna-Fuentes, J. (2007). Socioemtional wealth and business risks in family controlled firms: evidence from spanish olive oil mills. *Administrative Science Quarterly, 52*(1), 106–137.

Gomez-Mejia, L. R., Cruz, C., Berrone, P., & De Castro, J. (2011). The bind that ties: socioemotional wealth preservation in family firms. *The Academy of Management Annals, 5*(1), 653–707.

Gordon, G., & Nicholson, N. (2008). *Family wars: Stories and insights from famous family business feuds.* London, UK: Kogan Page.

Grant Thornton International. (n.d.). The Grant Thornton Family Business Centre website. Retrieved from http://www.gti.org/files/phb_succeeding_at_succession _overview.pdf

Grote, J. (2003). Conflicting generations: A new theory of family business rivalry. *Family Business Review, 16,* 113–124.

Habershon, T. G., Williams, M., & MacMillan, I. C. (2003). A unified systems perspective of family firm performance. *Journal of Business Venturing, 18,* 451–465.

Harris, L. C., & Ogbanna, E. (2005). Ownership and control in closely held family-owned firms: An exploration of strategic and operational control. *British Journal of Management, 18,* 5–26.

Hilburt-Davis, J., & Dyer, W. G. (2003). *Consulting to family business.* San Francisco, CA: Jossey-Bass.

H. E. Butt Foundation. (n.d.). H. E. Butt Foundation website. Retrieved from http://www.laityrenewal.org/aboutFoundation.php

History of the Hénokiens. (n.d.). Retrieved from http://www.henokiens.com/ index_histo_gb.php

Hoy, F., & Sharma, P. (2010). *Entrepreneurial family firms.* New York, NY: Prentice Hall

Ibrahim, N. A., Angelides, J. P., & Parsa, F. (2008). Strategic management of family businesses: Current findings and directions for future research. *International Journal of Management, 25*(1), 95–110.

Jorissen, A., Laveren, E., Martens, R., & Reheul, A.-M. (2005). Real versus sample-based differences in comparative family business research. *Family Business Review, 18*(3), 229–246.

Kachaner, N., Stalk, G., & Bloch, a., (November 2012). What you can learn from family business. *Harvard Business Review, 90*(11), 103–106.

Kakkonen, M. L. (2005). Intuition of family entrepreneurs: An exploratory study of perceptions and experiences. *Journal of Enterprising Culture, 13*(1), 47–67.

Kellermanns, F. W., & Eddleston, K. A. (2004). Feuding families: When conflict does a family firm good. *Entrepreneurship Theory and Practice, 28*, 209–228.

Kelly, L. M., Athanassiou, N., & Crittenden W. F. (2000). Founder centrality and strategic behavior in the family owned firm. *Entrepreneurship Theory and Practice, 25*, 27–42.

Kets de Vries, M. F. R. (1993). The dynamics of family controlled firms: The good and bad news. *Organizational Dynamics, 21*(3), 59–71.

KPMG. (2009). Family business survey 2009. Retrieved from http://www.kpmg .com/AU/en/IssuesAndInsights/ArticlesPublications/Documents/Family%20 Business%20Survey%202009.pdf

Kristies, L. (2008). The world's oldest family companies. *Family Business Magazine.* Retrieved from http://www.familybusinessmagazine.com/FBfiles/ worldsoldest.html

Kurashina, T. (2003). *Famiri kigyo no keieigaku* [Management of family business]. Tokyo, Japan: Toyo Keizai Shinposha.

Laird Norton Tyee. (2007). Family business survey: Family to family 2007. Retrieved from http://www.familybusinesssurvey.com

Landes, D. S. (2006). *Dynasties: Fortunes and misfortunes of the world's great family businesses.* New York, NY: Viking.

Leach, P., & Bogood, T. (1999). *Guide to the family business.* London: Kogan Page.

Le Breton-Miller, I., & Miller, D. (2015). The arts and family business: linking family business resources and performance to industry characteristics. *Entrepreneurship Theory and Practice, 39*(6), 1349–1370.

Lee, J. (2006a). Family firm performance: Further evidence. *Family Business Review, 19*(2), 103–114.

Lee, J. (2006b) Impact of family relationships on attitudes for the second generation in family businesses. *Family Business Review, 19*(3), 175-191

Levinson, H. (1971). Conflicts that plague the family business. *Harvard Business Review, 71*, 90–98.

Lindgren, H. (2002, August 22–24). *Succession strategies in a large family business group: The case of the Swedish Wallenberg Family.* Paper prepared for the 6th European Business History Association Annual Congress in Helsinki.

Lozano, M., Overbeke, K. K., & Alderson, K. (2011). *Father/Daughter Succession: A Case Study of a Colombian Family Business.* In D. Halkias, P. M. Swiercz, C. Smith, & R. S. Nason (Eds.). *Father daughter succession in family business: a cross-cultural perspective.* Aldershot, UK: Gower Publishing Ltd.

Martinez, J. I., Quiroga, B. F., & Stöhr, B. S. (2007, June). Family ownership and firm performance: Evidence from public companies in Chile. *Family Business Review, 20*(2), 83–94.

MassMutual Financial Group/Raymond Institute. (2002). *American family business survey*. Retrieved March 20, 2007, from http://kennesaw.edu/fec/DMD9500R.pdf

MassMutual Financial Group. (2007). *American family business survey.*

McCann, G. (2007). *When your parents sign the paychecks: Finding career success inside or outside the family business.* Indianapolis, IN: Jist Works.

McConaughy, D. L., Matthews, C. H., & Fialko, A. S. (2001). Founding family controlled firms: Performance, risk, and value. *Journal of Small Business Management, 39*(1), 31–49.

McIlhenny Corporation history. Retrieved from http://www.tabasco.com/tabasco_history/mcilhenny.cfm

Miller, D., & Le Breton-Miller, I. (2005a). Management insights from great and struggling family businesses. *Long Range Planning, 38*, 517–530.

Miller, D., & Le Breton-Miller, I. (2005b). *Managing for the long run: Lessons in competitive advantage from great family businesses.* Boston, MA: Harvard Business School Press.

Miller, D., Steier, L., & Le Breton-Miller, I. (2016). What can scholars of entrepreneurship learn from sound family businesses? *Entrepreneurship Theory and Practice, 40*(3), 445–455.

Murray, B., Gersick. K., & Lansberg, I. (2001/2002). From back office to executive suite-the evolving role of the family office. *Private Wealth Management,* 111–114. Retrieved from http://www.familybusinesssolutions.co.uk/UserFiles/File/FromBackOfficeToExecSuite.pdf

Mustakallio, M., Autio, E., & Zahra, S. (2002). Relational and contractual governance in family firms: Effects on strategic decision-making. *Family Business Review, 15*, 205–223.

Neal, J., & Vallejo, M. C. (2008). Family firms as incubators for spirituality in the workplace: Factors that nurture spiritual businesses. *Journal of Management, Spirituality & Religion, 5*(2), 115–159.

Niehm, L., Swinney, J., & Miller, N. J. (2008). Community social responsibility and its consequences for family business performance. *Journal of Small Business Management, 46*(3), 331–350.

Open innovation. (2010). Open innovation in the Arab family business: A must or an oxymoron? *Tharawat Magazine, 6.* Retrieved from http://tharawat.org/research.php

Overview. (2008). *Overview of family business relevant issues-final report.* Brussels, Belgium: European Commission, Enterprise and Industry, Directorate-General.

Passing. (2004, November 4). Passing on the crown. *The Economist.* Retrieved from http://www.economist.com/node/3352686?story_id=3352686

Pawar, S. (2009, August). Family business in India: Future of family business. *Business and Management Chronicle.* Retrieved from http://www.scribd.com/doc/16691629/Family-Business-in-India

Pearl, J. A. (2010, spring). Pruning the family tree. *Family Business Magazine, 21*(2), 61–64.

Pearl. J. A., & Kristies, L. (2009). The world's largest family businesses. *Family Business Magazine, 20*(2). Retrieved from http://www.familybusinessmagazine.com/index.php?/channels/articles/the_worlds_largest_family_businesses

Piliso, S. (2006, April 23). South Africa: Number of family businesses soars to over the million mark. *Sunday Times.* Retrieved from http://allafrica.com/stories/200604240732.html

Picchi, A. (May 11, 2017). *Meet america's newest billionaire, millennial lynsi snyder.* CBS Moneywatch. Retrieved from http://ey.com/Publication/vwLU-Assets/ey-women-in-leadership-the-family-business-advantage/$FILE/ey-women-in-leadership-the-family-business-advantage.pdf

Pindado, J., & Requejo, I. (2015). Family business performance from a governance perspective: a review of empirical research. *International Journal of Management Reviews, 17*(3), 279–311.

Poza, E. J. (2009). *Family business* (3rd ed.). Mason, OH: Thomson South-Western.

Poza, E. J. (2007). *Family business* (2nd ed.). Mason OH: Thomson South-Western.

PricewaterhouseCoopers (2007/2008). *Making a difference: The PricewaterhouseCoopers family business survey.* Retrieved from http://www.pwc.com

Prince, R. A., & File, K. M. (1996). Marketing professional services to family businesses. *Journal of Professional Services Marketing, 15*(1), 121–135.

Prince, R. A., & File, K. M. (1995). *Marketing to family business owners: A toolkit for life insurance professionals.* Cincinnati, OH: National Underwriter.

PWC. (2015). US Family Business Survey. Retrieved from https://pwc.com/us/en/private-company-services/publications/2015-family-business-survey.html

Revilla, A. J., Perez-Luno, A., & Nieto, M. J. (2016). Does family involvement in management reduce the risk of business failure? The moderating role of entrepreneurial orientation. *Family Business Review, 29*(4), 365–379.

Sanyal, R., & Dutt, D. (2010, January 27). *Barclays wealth launches family business forum in India.* Retrieved from http://www.barclayswealth.com/about-us/news/barclays-wealth-launches-family-business-forum-in-india.htm

SC Johnson website. Retrieved from http://www.scjohnson.com/en/company/principles.aspx

Schulze, W. S., Lubatkin, M. H., Dino, R. N., & Buchholtz, A. K. (2001). Agency relationships in family firms: Theory and evidence. *Organization Science, 12*(2), 99–116.

Schroeder, A. (2008) *Snowball: Warren Buffett and the business of life.* New York, NY: Random House.

Sellers, P. (September 16, 2014). Fortune Magazine. Retrieved from http://fortune.com/2014/09/16/secretive-heir-heineken/

Sharma, P. (2004). An overview of the field of family business studies: Current status and directions for the future. *Family Business Review, 17,* 1–36.

Sharma, P., Chrisman, J. J., & Chua, J. H. (1996). *A review and annotated bibliography of family business studies.* Boston, MA: Kluwer Academic.

Sharma, P., & Irving, P. G. (2005). Four bases of family business successor commitment: Antecedents and consequences. *Entrepreneurship Theory and Practice, 29*(1), 13–33.

Sharma P., & Manikutty, S. (2005). Strategic divestment in family firms: Role of family structure and community culture. *Entrepreneurship Theory and Practice, 29,* 293–311.

Shearman & Sterling, LLC. (2017). JD Supra. Retrieved 12/29/17 from https://jdsupra.com/legalnews/tax-reform-summary-for-family-offices-29409/

Shepherd, D. A., & Zacharakis, A. (2000). Structuring family business succession: An analysis of the future leader's decision making. *Entrepreneurship Theory and Practice, 24*(4), 25–41.

Sirmon, D. G., & Hitt, M. A. (2003, summer). Managing resources: Linking unique resources management and wealth creation in family firms. *Entrepreneurship Theory and Practice,* 339–358.

Stewart, A., & Hitt, M. A. (2012). Why can't a family business be more like a nonfamily business?: Modes of professionalization in family firms. *Family Business Review, 25*(1), 58–86.

Sonfield, M. C., & Lussier, R. N. (2004). First, second, and third generation family firms: A comparison. *Family Business Review, 17,* 189–202.

Stavrou, E. (1999). Succession in family businesses: Exploring the effects of demographic factors on offspring intentions to join and take over the firm. *Journal of Small Business Management, 37*(3), 43-61.

Still keeping. (2004, March 18). Still keeping it in the family: Business in Mexico. *The Economist.* Retrieved from http://www.economist.com/node/2523586

Stroh, F. (2016). *Beer money: A memoir of privilege and loss.* Harper Collins, NY.

Susanto, A. B., & Susanto, P. (2013). *The dragon network: inside stories of the most successful chinese family businesses.* Bloomberg Press, NY.

Tagiuri, R., & Davis, J. A. (1996). Bivalent attributes of the family firm. *Family Business Review, 9*, 199–208.

The richest. (2010, October 11). The richest people in America. *Forbes, 186*(6).

Tripathi, D. (1999, October). *Change & continuity.* A symposium on the role of the family in Indian business. Retrieved from http://www.india-seminar.com/1999/482/482%20tripathi.htm

Upton, N. B., & Felan, J. (2001, February 2–3). *Fast-growth family firms: Lessons from the Gazelles, conference book for Stetson University's second annual family business gathering,* Deland, Florida.

Venter, E., Boshoff, C., & Maas, G. (2003). The influence of relational factors on successful succession in family businesses: A comparative study of owner-managers and successors. *South African Journal of Business Management, 34*(4), 1–13.

Vera, C. F., & Dean, M. A. (2005). An examination of the challenges daughters face in family business succession. *Family Business Review, 18*(4), 321–345.

Wallop, H. (January 1, 2013). They're 300 years old and still in business. *The Telegraph.* Retrieved from http://telegraph.co.uk/finance/yourbusiness/9772950/Theyre-300-years-old-and-still-in-business.html

Wang, Y. (2010). A report on the IFERA@CHINA 2010 Family Business Forum: Opportunities and challenges of family business. Wolverhampton Business School, United Kingdom, on behalf of IFERA@CHINA. Retrieved from http://www.ifera.org/index.php?option=com_content&view=article&id=103:ifera-china-2010-family-business-forum&catid=46:forums&Itemid=112

Ward, J. L. (2004) *Perpetuating the family business. 50 Lessons learned from long-lasting successful families in business.* New York, NY: Palgrave Macmillan.

Ward, J. L. (1986). *Keeping the family business healthy.* New York: NY: Jossey-Bass.

Welsch, J. (1996). The impact of family ownership and involvement on the process of management succession. In R. Beckhard (Ed.), *The best of FBR: A celebration* (pp. 96–108). Boston, MA: Family Firm Institute.

Westhead, P., & Cowling, M. (1998). Family firm research: The need for a methodological rethink. *Entrepreneurship Theory and Practice, 23*(1), 31–56.

WinShape Foundation. Retrieved from http://www.winshape.org/

Index

OTHER TITLES IN THE ENTREPRENEURSHIP AND SMALL BUSINESS MANAGEMENT COLLECTION

Scott Shane, Case Western University, Editor

- *Open Innovation Essentials for Small and Medium Enterprises: A Guide to Help Entrepreneurs in Adopting the Open Innovation Paradigm in Their Business* by Luca Escoffier, Adriano La Vopa, Phyllis Speser, and Daniel Satinsky
- *The Technological Entrepreneur's Playbook* by Ian Chaston
- *Licensing Myths & Mastery: Why Most Ideas Don't Work and What to Do About It* by William S. Seidel
- *Arts and Entrepreneurship* by J. Mark Munoz and Julie Shields
- *The Human Being's Guide to Business Growth: A Simple Process for Unleashing the Power of Your People for Growth* by Gregory Scott Chambers

Announcing the Business Expert Press Digital Library

Concise e-books business students need for classroom and research

This book can also be purchased in an e-book collection by your library as

- a one-time purchase,
- that is owned forever,
- allows for simultaneous readers,
- has no restrictions on printing, and
- can be downloaded as PDFs from within the library community.

Our digital library collections are a great solution to beat the rising cost of textbooks. E-books can be loaded into their course management systems or onto students' e-book readers.
The **Business Expert Press** digital libraries are very affordable, with no obligation to buy in future years. For more information, please visit **www.businessexpertpress.com/librarians**. To set up a trial in the United States, please email **sales@businessexpertpress.com**.